The Easier Way to Knit

A Guide to Double Rake Loom Knitting for All Skill Levels

Kera Weiserbs

Copyright © 2017 by Kera Weiserbs

All rights reserved. The written instructions, photographs, designs, patterns, charts, original stitches, and projects in this volume may not be reproduced without the author's permission.

Printed by CreateSpace Independent Publishing Platform

ISBN-10: 1545040516; ISBN-13: 978-1545040515
Library of Congress Control Number: 2017909218

Table of contents

Acknowledgements iii

Preface iv

Double rake looms.. 1

    Introduction 1

    Looping diagrams and conventions.............. 2

Learn to double knit 4

    Casting on.. 4

    Weaving a stitch pattern 8

    Knitting stitches... 8

    Binding off.. 9

    Loom knitting tips 12

Double knit fabrics 13

    Loop structure 13

    Slip stitches & fabric elasticity..................... 14

    Using beads to track structure..................... 15

    Exploring stitch modifications 15

    Gauge... 16

    Yarn estimator 19

Knitting charts 21

    Knitoglyphics.. 21

    Interpreting knitting charts........................... 22

    Crosses 23

        Loop crosses 23

        Stitch crosses 24

        Knitting charts with crosses.................. 24

    Compound stitches 26

Knitting techniques 27

    Changing yarns...27

    Shaping 28

    Buttonholes...29

    Seaming...30

Color knitting..31

    Introduction to color theory........................31

    Basic color techniques..................................32

    Advanced color knitting techniques............34

        Intarsia...34

        Simple brioche.......................................35

        Stranded knitting...................................36

        Knitting with beads...............................38

Stitches 40

    Basic stitches..41

    Rib stitches...48

    Brioche stitches 59

    Fretwork stitches 67

Index 72

Acknowledgements

Many people helped me with this book, and I want to thank them for their support and assistance. I am especially grateful for helpful suggestions from my mother, Barbara Weiserbs, my editor, Joanne Grumet, and Vanessa Velez DeGarcia, a friend and professional photographer. My mother read the original manuscript and had great advice for improving the text. Without her help, the book would have been more technical and harder to read. I am also very thankful for Joanne Grumet, who carefully reviewed every chapter. Her advice was always thoughtful and improved the text. I also need to thank Vanessa Velez DeGarcia for testing the knitting instructions. I'm grateful for everyone's help.

I am very appreciative of the help I received from Sharlette Cook. Sharlette is a fantastic knitter, weaver, and spinner. Sharlette's help was invaluable. In addition to encouraging me to write this series, Sharlette spent time answering my questions about knitting terminology, stitches, and cables. We enjoyed looking through her knitting library and inventing names for new stitches.

I especially want to thank my daughter, Elizabeth Lee, who is a great colorist. Thank you for being so tolerant and patient as I deliberated in every yarn store we went to. Lastly, I want to thank my husband Ti-Kuang Lee for his encouragement, help, and for setting up rakeknitting.com.

Preface

Why use the double rake knitting loom?

The **double rake loom** is a knitting tool composed of two rows of pegs that function as multiple knitting needles to create **double knit fabrics**. Double knit fabrics are two layer thick, reversible fabrics that are formed by interlocking the "wrong" side of two single knit fabrics. **Interlocking** hides knots, color changes and non-decorative stitches on the "wrong" side of a fabric and produces a strong woven fabric that prevents stretching, wrinkling, and curled edges. These attributes make double knitting especially useful for projects that are reversible, use multiple colors, or are visible from both sides.

While knitting needles are the most common method of creating double knit fabric, the double rake loom has several advantages over knitting needles. The structure of the loom makes it much easier to knit evenly spaced stitches than knitting needles, especially for beginning knitters. The loom's structure also allows placement of a knitting template next to the pegs, which facilitates color knitting and beading. Rake knitting requires less fine motor skill and uses fewer repetitive movements than knitting needles; therefore, it is a great knitting choice for children and people with wrist, hand, and/or repetitive motion problems.

Despite the many advantages of rake knitting, it also has drawbacks. The base hides several rows of stitches, which can make it hard to count stitches and detect errors. Fabric width is limited by the length of the rakes, and there are far fewer knitting patterns for rake knitting than for traditional needle knitting. The growing popularity of loom knitting and the associated increase in loom knitting resources are decreasing these challenges.

What was the motivation for writing this book?

I started working on this book for several reasons. First, I wanted to understand how the loom forms double knit fabrics, but I couldn't find resources that explained the process. As I worked on understanding the process, I thought this would interest other loom knitters. Second, a knitting chart system for double rake knitting was needed. Traditional knitting charts are not suitable for double rake knitting because they only represent one-sided fabric, and double knit fabrics have two sides. To remedy this, I developed a knitting chart system that includes rake specific instructions. Third, there are very few books on double rake loom knitting, and no book explains how to knit more than twenty different stitches. In contrast, this book illustrates how to knit thirty-eight different stitches, including eleven original stitches.

Moreover, the presentation of these stitches is unique. In addition to standard presentation methods, such as photos of swatches or peg wrap sequences, this book also uses looping diagrams and knitting charts that illustrate how to knit stitches with multiple steps. Although uncommon in the loom knitting literature, these summary illustrations are a great resource for quickly replicating stitches, and in my opinion, they are the easiest way to learn and to record stitches.

Enjoy double knitting with your double rake loom!

Kera

Double rake looms

Introduction

The **double rake loom** (a.k.a. knitting board, long loom, rectangular loom, Mayan loom, or Aztec loom) is a hand knitting tool that creates double knit fabrics without a lot of practice. This loom consists of two rows of evenly spaced pegs that function as multiple knitting needles, which create evenly spaced stitches. Figure 1 and Figure 2 are examples of double rake looms with fixed and adjustable rakes respectively. The distance between the rakes influences the fabric's **gauge** or stitch density, the number of rows and stitches per centimeter or inch.

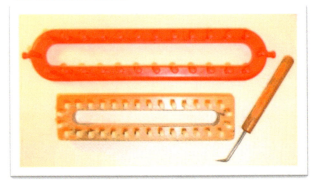

Figure 1: Double rake looms with fixed space between the rakes.

Figure 2: Double rake loom with adjustable spacers between the rakes and a loom hook tool.

Any rigid tubing can be used to adjust the distance between adjustable rakes. However, stacked washers are the most accurate way of modifying gauge, since they can be incrementally stacked. Fewer washers reduce the space between the rakes, which forms shorter stitches, and more washers increase the space between the rakes and form longer stitches.

Regardless of the gauge, a main advantage of the double rake loom is the even stitches produced by the loom's evenly spaced pegs. Figure 3 illustrates how the even spacing between pegs creates even stitches.

Figure 3: The structure of the pegs creates even spacing between loops.

Looping diagrams and conventions

Double knit fabric is created on a double rake loom by weaving a stitch pattern around the pegs and knitting the loops together. The easiest way to illustrate a stitch pattern is with a **looping diagram**. A looping diagram is a representation of a double rake loom where the pegs (Figure 4) are replaced by circles in (Figure 5). Looping diagrams illustrate where the pattern begins and how the yarn wraps around the pegs.

Figure 5 shows the looping diagram for the stockinette stitch, the most common double knit stitch. The blue forward wrap of this looping pattern begins on peg 1 on the back rake (**BR**) and weaves around the outside of each catty-corner peg until the last peg where the yarn is woven across to the opposite rake. The red return wrap follows the same pattern as the blue forward wrap but in the opposite direction. Although the looping pattern for the stockinette stitch is relatively straightforward, to help clarify more complicated patterns, each looping diagram is accompanied with separate forward and return wraps, such as Figure 6.

Figure 4: Double rake loom.

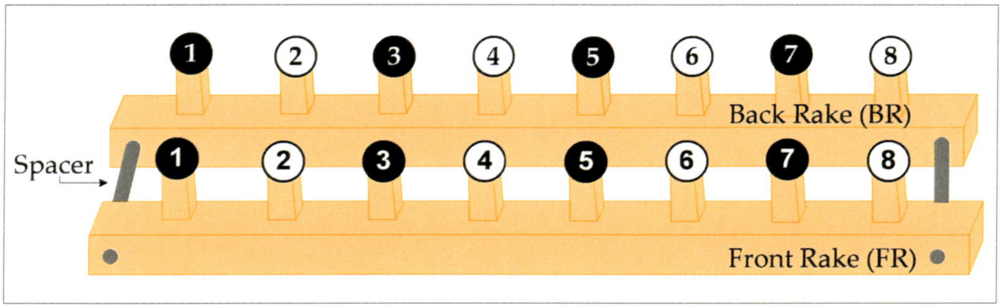

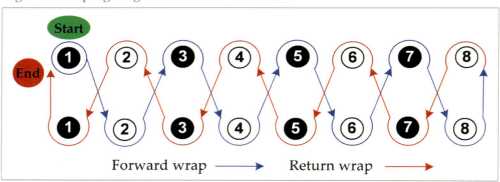

Figure 5: Looping diagram for the stockinette stitch.

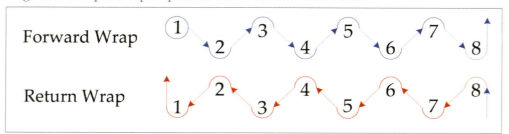

Figure 6: Sample wrap sequences for the stockinette stitch.

2 · The Easier Way to Knit

In each looping diagram, the forward wrap begins with a **slip knot** that attaches the yarn to a peg. The slip knot, which is explained in detail on the next page, is represented by a blue, open circle. The forward wrap is illustrated in blue, and the return wrap is illustrated in red. These looping diagram conventions are illustrated in Figure 7. In addition, the back and front rakes are abbreviated as **FR** and **BR** respectively.

Figure 7: Looping diagram conventions.

Loop types

Loops are formed by weaving yarn around the pegs with either a **u-wrap** or an **e-wrap**. These wraps are aptly named for the way the yarn forms a 'u' or a script 'e' around pegs. Figure 8 illustrates these wraps on a 2-peg, double rake loom. The u-wrap creates flatter stitches than the curvier e-wrap. Figure 9 illustrates swatches and loop diagrams for the stockinette and twisted stockinette stitches; these are two stitches that use the same pattern, which weaves around the outside of each catty-corner peg, but different loop wraps. The stockinette stitch is knit with u-wraps and the twisted stockinette is knit with e-wraps.

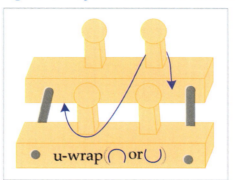
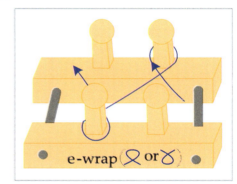

Figure 8: Wraps for the double rake loom.

Figure 9: The effect of e- vs u-wrapping the stockinette stitch.

Stitch	Stockinette	Twisted Stockinette
Wrap	u-wrapped stockinette stitch u-wrap (∩ or ∪)	e-wrapped stockinette stitch e-wrap (ℯ or ℯ)
Loop diagram		
Swatch		

Double rake looms · 3

Learn to double knit

Casting on

Knitting begins by **casting on**, the process of forming the first row of loops on a knitted fabric. These loops are distinct from subsequent loops because they are connected to the fabric by only one set of stitches, while most other loops are connected to both a preceding and a succeeding stitch.

To cast on, attach the yarn to a peg with a slip knot. Figure 10 demonstrates one way to form a slip knot. Start by unwinding 12 inches of yarn (a **yarn tail**); form a pretzel by folding the yarn tail in half and under the loop (A); bring the yarn tail over the small loop (B) and then under it (C); lastly, pull on the main strand (D) to tighten the knot.

Double rake knitting requires ONLY 4 steps

1. Casting on
2. Weaving a stitch pattern
3. Knitting stitches
4. Binding off

Figure 10: How to make a slip knot.

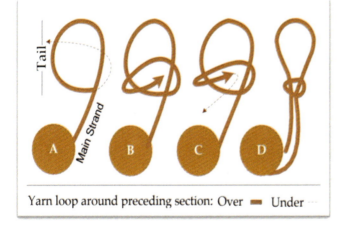

Once the yarn is attached to the loom with a slip knot, weave a row of cast-on stitches. Either select one of the recommended cast-on stitches, which accompanies the knitting instruction for each stitch (in the *Stitch Section*) or experiment with other stitches. The stockinette stitch (Figure 11) and the zigzag stitch (Figure 14) are the most common cast-on stitches. Figure 11 illustrates how to cast on with the stockinette stitch. After weaving the stockinette stitch around the loom, add an **anchor**. An anchor is a piece of yarn or a stick that secures the cast-on row, helps the fabric move evenly between the rakes, and helps with **binding off**. Binding off is the process that closes **live ends** (stitches with an unattached edge), such as the first and the last row of stitches, by adding a decorative edge.

Figure 11: How to cast on with the stockinette stitch.

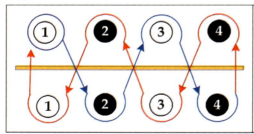

1. Add a slip knot to peg 1 on the BR;
2. Wrap the pegs with a row of the stockinette stitch;
3. Add an anchor (See instruction on the next page).

4 · The Easier Way to Knit

Anchor yarn

An **anchor yarn** is a piece of yarn that is tied around the cast-on stitches. The anchor yarn should be 2.5 times the length of the wrap sequence. It is best to use yarn that contrasts the knitted fabric because a contrasting color is easy to see and will help facilitate binding off the live end. After adding an anchor yarn, pull on the anchor after completing each row of stitches, crosses, or beads; this helps form even stitches. Figure 12 shows how to cast on and use an anchor yarn.

Anchor stick

Casting on with an **anchor stick** is an alternative to casting on with yarn. To cast on with an anchor stick, place a stick, such as a bamboo skewer, a metal rod, or a narrow dowel that is at least an inch longer than the cast-on sequence, on top of the cast-on pattern. Initially, the anchor stick needs to be pushed down between the rakes. However, once the anchor stick descends below the rake, pull it after knitting each row. If the space between the rakes is too narrow for your fingers, add a yarn strand to both ends of the anchor stick and pull on the yarn strands until the anchor descends below the rake and can be pulled. Figure 13 shows how to cast on and use an anchor stick. I prefer the anchor stick method because it produces a more even edge than an anchor yarn, and it facilitates binding off (See Figure 19).

Figure 12: Casting on with an anchor yarn.

Figure 13: Casting on with an anchor stick.

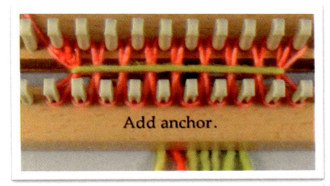

Add anchor.

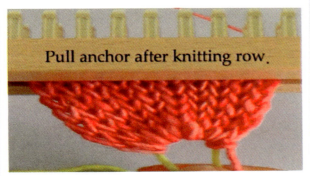

Pull anchor after knitting row.

After completing the first rotation of the cast on stitch, add an anchor stick.

After knitting the 1st row of stitches, push the stick between rakes.

Multiple rows of stitches: Pull anchor stick after completing each row of stitches.

Learn to double knit · 5

Tight cast-on

As the name suggests, a tight cast-on creates a tighter edge than other cast-on methods. Instructions for the tight cast-on are separated into two parts: Figure 14 illustrates how to weave the zigzag stitch for a tight cast-on, and Figure 15 illustrates how to remove the excess yarn, which tightens the stitches. Before weaving the zigzag stitch, add a slip knot onto a temporary holding peg, a peg adjacent to the first peg in your wrap sequence, (in Figure 14, the temporary holding peg is labeled peg 0) and work clockwise around peg 1 on the back rake (BR). Second, wrap the pegs with the forward wrap of the zigzag stitch by weaving the yarn down to the left of peg 1 on the FR and counterclockwise around it. Thereafter, weave the yarn up to the left of and clockwise around the next peg on the BR and counterclockwise on the FR until the last peg. Third, add an anchor stick and the return wrap of the zigzag stitch. To begin the return wrap, bring the yarn straight across to the BR and weave the yarn in the opposite direction. Now, each loop begins on the right side of each peg and alternates between counterclockwise loops on the BR and clockwise loops on the FR.

Figure 15 shows how to remove the excess yarn from a tight zigzag cast-on. Removing the excess yarn is a multistep process. First, add a stitch to the first peg on the FR by **knitting off** the bottom loop over its peg (See Figure 17 for detailed instructions on how to knit off); second, beginning with the right-most loop on the BR, use the loom hook tool (a.k.a. hook tool) to gather the excess yarn around the bottom (blue) loop. Working from right to left, repeat this process for each peg on the BR. To remove the excess yarn from peg 1, remove the slip knot and pull the yarn tail tautly. If the anchor stick has moved, adjust it so that it lies parallel to the rakes. Lastly, knit off loop pairs on the BR, beginning with peg 1 and continuing to the right.

Loom hook tool

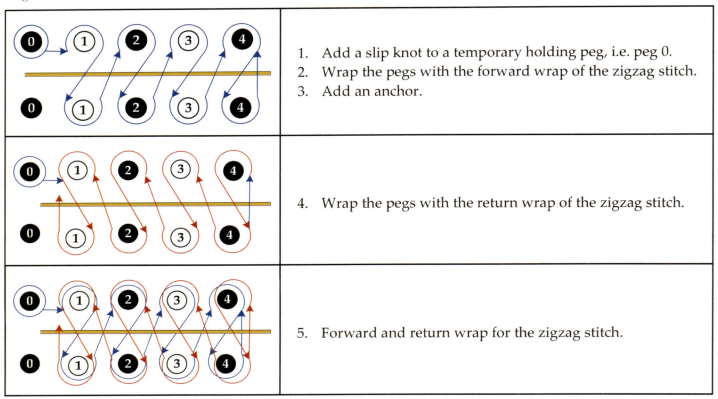

Figure 14: Instructions for weaving the zigzag stitch for a tight cast-on.

1. Add a slip knot to a temporary holding peg, i.e. peg 0.
2. Wrap the pegs with the forward wrap of the zigzag stitch.
3. Add an anchor.

4. Wrap the pegs with the return wrap of the zigzag stitch.

5. Forward and return wrap for the zigzag stitch.

6 · The Easier Way to Knit

Figure 15: Instructions for removing excess yarn from a zigzag cast-on.

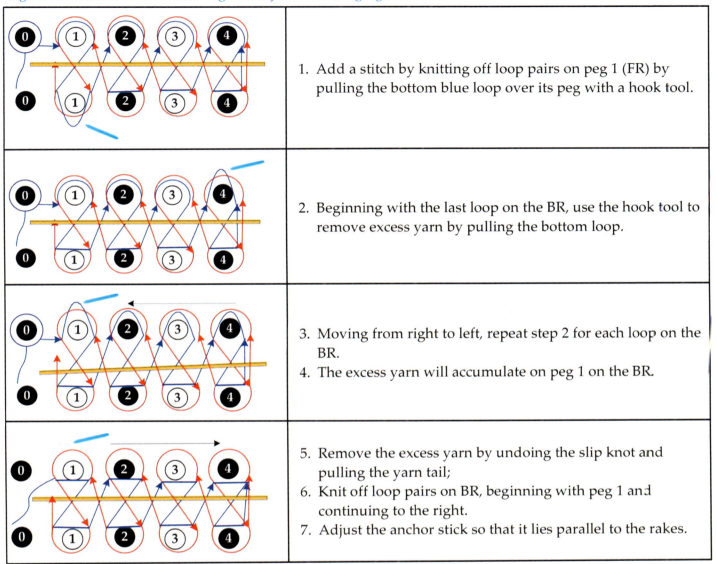

1. Add a stitch by knitting off loop pairs on peg 1 (FR) by pulling the bottom blue loop over its peg with a hook tool.

2. Beginning with the last loop on the BR, use the hook tool to remove excess yarn by pulling the bottom loop.

3. Moving from right to left, repeat step 2 for each loop on the BR.
4. The excess yarn will accumulate on peg 1 on the BR.

5. Remove the excess yarn by undoing the slip knot and pulling the yarn tail;
6. Knit off loop pairs on BR, beginning with peg 1 and continuing to the right.
7. Adjust the anchor stick so that it lies parallel to the rakes.

Learn to double knit · 7

Casting on with fringe
Advanced topic

Fringe can be used to cast on to the loom or added after knitting. Instructions for casting on with fringe are summarized in Figure 16.

Figure 16: Instructions for casting on with fringe.

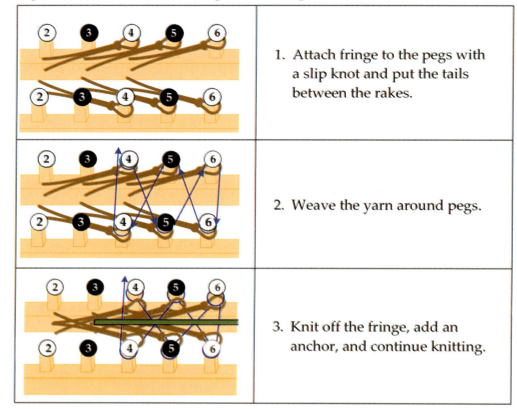

1. Attach fringe to the pegs with a slip knot and put the tails between the rakes.

2. Weave the yarn around pegs.

3. Knit off the fringe, add an anchor, and continue knitting.

Weaving a stitch pattern

This section explains how to weave the stockinette stitch. In addition, the chapter on *stitches* explains how to weave an additional thirty-seven stitches. Each stitch in that chapter includes a swatch, a summary of its uses and decorative characteristics, written directions, and a looping diagram that illustrates how to weave the stitch around the loom.

Knitting stitches

Once the yarn is cast on to the loom, you can begin knitting. Figure 17 illustrates how to knit a two-stitch wide chain. In this diagram, the blue line represents the first rows of stockinette loops, and the red line represents the second row of stockinette loops. The blue line is dashed when it is beneath a red loop and solid when it is knit over a red loop. To form a stitch, pull the bottom blue loop (A) over its peg (B) with a hook tool. This creates one stitch (C) and is termed "**knitting off**." The last diagram (D) represents a **row of stitches**.

Figure 17: Knitting instructions.

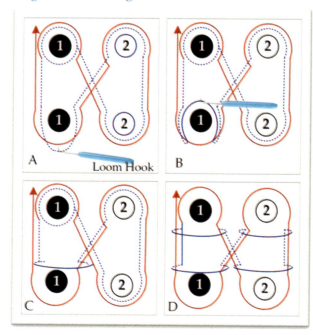

8 · The Easier Way to Knit

Binding off

Binding off removes live ends by adding a decorative edge. Figure 18 contains swatches for two different bind-off techniques: the narrow crochet bind-off and the elastic loom hook bind-off.

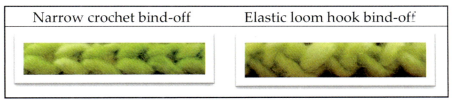

Figure 18: Sample bind-offs.

Narrow crochet bind-off

Instructions for adding a narrow crochet bind-off are illustrated in Figure 19. This bind-off creates a very even and decorative edge that is difficult to undo.

Figure 19: Instructions for a narrow crochet bind-off.

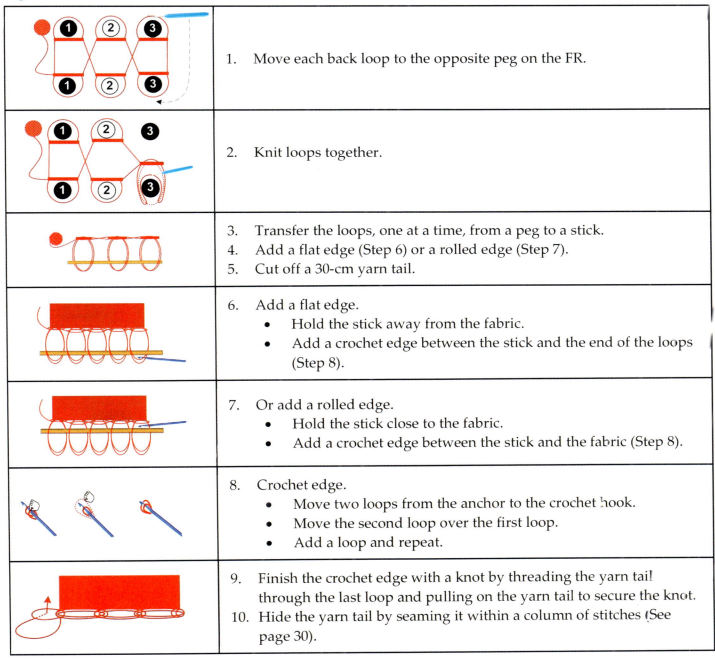

1. Move each back loop to the opposite peg on the FR.
2. Knit loops together.
3. Transfer the loops, one at a time, from a peg to a stick.
4. Add a flat edge (Step 6) or a rolled edge (Step 7).
5. Cut off a 30-cm yarn tail.
6. Add a flat edge.
   - Hold the stick away from the fabric.
   - Add a crochet edge between the stick and the end of the loops (Step 8).
7. Or add a rolled edge.
   - Hold the stick close to the fabric.
   - Add a crochet edge between the stick and the fabric (Step 8).
8. Crochet edge.
   - Move two loops from the anchor to the crochet hook.
   - Move the second loop over the first loop.
   - Add a loop and repeat.
9. Finish the crochet edge with a knot by threading the yarn tail through the last loop and pulling on the yarn tail to secure the knot.
10. Hide the yarn tail by seaming it within a column of stitches (See page 30).

Learn to double knit · 9

Elastic loom hook bind-off

The elastic loom hook bind-off is shown in Figure 20; this bind-off method forms a crisscross edge that is often added to elastic garments.

Figure 20: Instructions for the elastic loom hook bind-off.

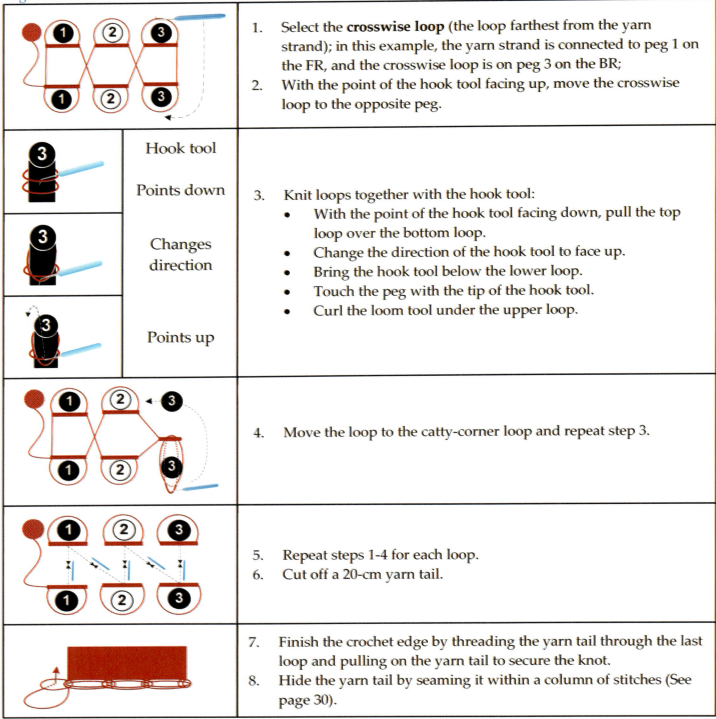

(diagram)		1. Select the **crosswise loop** (the loop farthest from the yarn strand); in this example, the yarn strand is connected to peg 1 on the FR, and the crosswise loop is on peg 3 on the BR; 2. With the point of the hook tool facing up, move the crosswise loop to the opposite peg.
(diagram)	Hook tool Points down Changes direction Points up	3. Knit loops together with the hook tool: • With the point of the hook tool facing down, pull the top loop over the bottom loop. • Change the direction of the hook tool to face up. • Bring the hook tool below the lower loop. • Touch the peg with the tip of the hook tool. • Curl the loom tool under the upper loop.
(diagram)		4. Move the loop to the catty-corner loop and repeat step 3.
(diagram)		5. Repeat steps 1-4 for each loop. 6. Cut off a 20-cm yarn tail.
(diagram)		7. Finish the crochet edge by threading the yarn tail through the last loop and pulling on the yarn tail to secure the knot. 8. Hide the yarn tail by seaming it within a column of stitches (See page 30).

10 · The Easier Way to Knit

Binding-off with fringe
Advanced topic

A fringe bind-off is another finishing option. Instructions for binding-off with fringe are illustrated in Figure 21. Fringe can also be added to a finished fabric by inserting yarn strands into stitches, instead of loops, and following the instructions in steps 2-5.

Figure 21: Instructions for binding off with fringe.

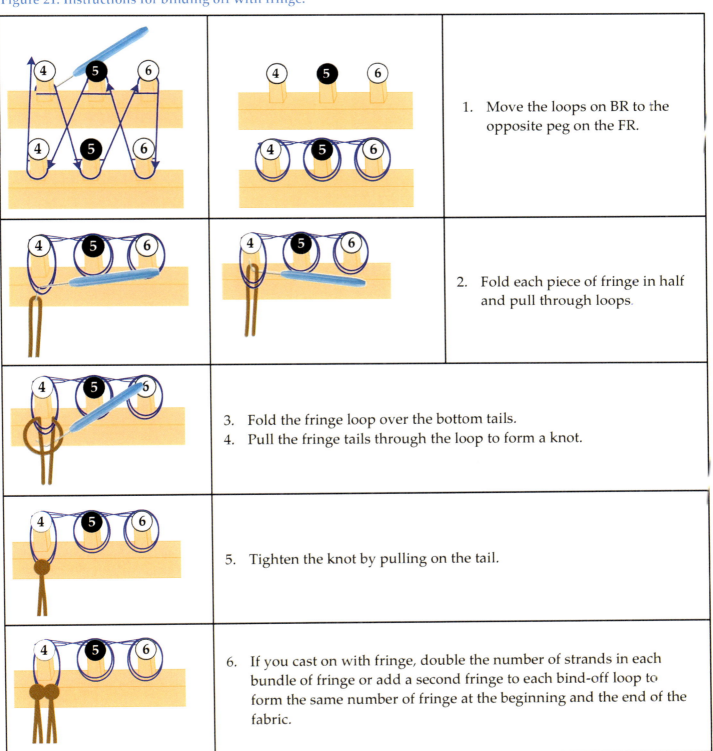

1. Move the loops on BR to the opposite peg on the FR.
2. Fold each piece of fringe in half and pull through loops.
3. Fold the fringe loop over the bottom tails.
4. Pull the fringe tails through the loop to form a knot.
5. Tighten the knot by pulling on the tail.
6. If you cast on with fringe, double the number of strands in each bundle of fringe or add a second fringe to each bind-off loop to form the same number of fringe at the beginning and the end of the fabric.

Learn to double knit · 11

Loom knitting tips

Although it is easier to form even stitches on the double rake loom than with knitting needles, inconsistent **tension** (tightness around the pegs) can cause tighter or looser stitches. Inconsistent tension is more problematic on longer looms (over 45 cm or 18 in. long) than on shorter looms; however, you can help maintain even tension by knitting loosely. In addition to maintaining even tension, knitting loosely also facilitates loop and stitch crosses because it is easier to move loose yarn over pegs. There are three knitting techniques that will help wrap yarn loosely and evenly around pegs. First and most importantly, always maintain a loose yarn strand by unwinding the ball of yarn as you knit. Second, hold the yarn loosely. Third, weave the yarn through a **stylus**, a hollow tube or straw; a stylus helps maintain even tension, increases peg wrapping speed, and helps prevent multiple yarn strands from twisting. Figure 22 demonstrates how to use a stylus. If uneven tension is still a problem, try the tips below.

Figure 22: Loom knitting stylus.

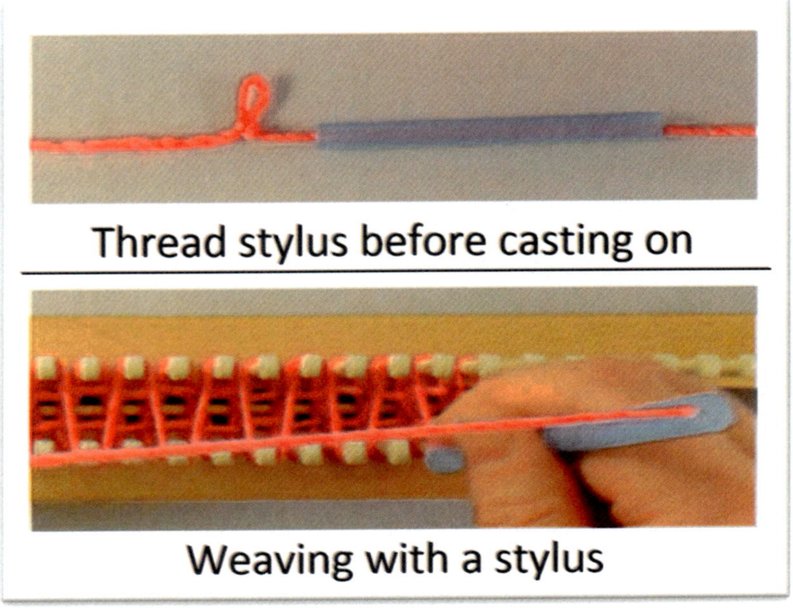

Thread stylus before casting on

Weaving with a stylus

Tips (in order of importance):

1. For stitches that require both a forward and a return wrap to complete (e.g., the stockinette stitch)
   a. Knit the last looped peg first and tighten the stitch by pulling on the main strand (the strand that you are knitting with).
   b. Knit off ten stitches at time, alternating between the right and left side of the loom. In other words, first, knit off the last looped peg (e.g., peg 40 and the nine adjacent stitches on both rakes, pegs 31-39); second, repeat the process, alternating between the right-most (e.g., pegs 1-10) and the left-most sides of the loom (e.g., pegs 21-30). When using this approach, the last knitted stitch should occur in the middle of the loom.

2. For stitches that only require one wrap to complete (e.g., the zigzag stitch)
   a. Knit off each peg as you loop them, instead of knitting off after looping all the pegs.

3. Additional tips
   a. Hold the hook tool away from the peg when looping stitches.
   b. Press the previous peg while wrapping the current peg.
   c. Before knitting off, loosen the tension in the previous stitch by slightly pulling it with the looping tool.

Double knit fabrics

Loop structure

Although you can knit without understanding the structure of double knit fabric, understanding the structure helped me feel more comfortable knitting on the double rake loom, so I am presenting it here.

Figure 23 illustrates the structure of one row of double knit stockinette stitches. Two colors of yarn (red and blue) help illustrate how **slip stitches** interlock loops by crossing between the loops that are formed on each peg. Figure 24 schematically illustrates a single row of double knit stockinette stitches. The stitches are represented by circles, and the slip stitches are represented by lines. This row of stitches also helps clarify how several rows of stitches are interconnected in Figure 25.

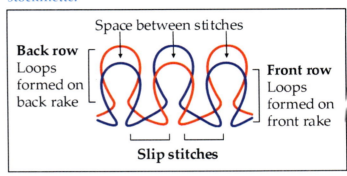

Figure 23: Structure of one row of double knit stockinette.

Figure 25 compares two rows of single and double knit stockinette and illustrates how new loops are pulled through old loops. The two-dimensional structure of a single knit stockinette is much easier to visualize than the more complex three-dimensional loop structure of double knit stockinette. To help visualize the three-dimensional structure of the double knit stockinette, trace the outline of one color across a row of stitches. Notice that within each column of stitches or "**wale**," new stitches are pulled through old stitches on the same side of the fabric as the previous stitches. However, in each row or "**course**" or "**weft**," slip stitches cross between the front and the back of the fabric, which forces the red and blue stitches to alternate between the front and back of each column.

Figure 24: Schematic illustration of one row of double knit stockinette.

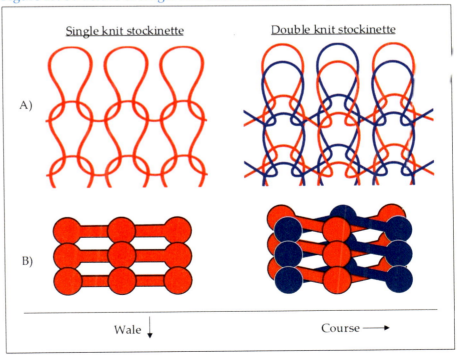

Figure 25: Structure of single and double knit stockinette fabric.

Slip stitches & fabric elasticity

On the double rake loom, slip stitches are formed by weaving yarn between the rakes. The slip stitch strengthens the structure of double knit fabrics and can be used to predict the stitch's elasticity. Figure 26 compares the slip stitches and their associated **cross angles** (the angle between slip stitches) for the stockinette stitch, the English stitch, and the single rib stitch. Stitches that use different pegs for the forward and return wraps, such as the stockinette stitch, have large cross angles and are more rigid than stitches that use the same pegs for both their forward and return wraps, such as the English and the single rib stitches. As expected, the single rib stitch, which has the smallest cross angle, is the most elastic of the three stitches in Figure 26.

Figure 26: Slip stitches for three stitches

Stockinette stitch	English stitch	Single rib stitch

Slip stitches are highlighted with dashed lines. ∠ Angle between slip stitches.

The effect of cross angle size on elasticity is illustrated with a rubber band held with four fingers versus a rubber band held with two fingers. Figure 27 demonstrates that a rubber band held with four fingers (column A) has a larger cross angle and is more rigid than a rubber band held with two fingers (columns B and C). This example is analogous to the stockinette stitch whose rigid slip stitches are connected to four pegs. The middle band, which is only held with two fingers, has a much smaller cross angle and is much more elastic than the rubber band held with four fingers. Similarly, the English and the single rib stitches, which have slip stitches that are only connected to two pegs, are much more elastic than the stockinette stitch. Lastly, the string without a cross angle that is held with two fingers is the most flexible.

Figure 27: String elasticity depends on the size of the cross angle.

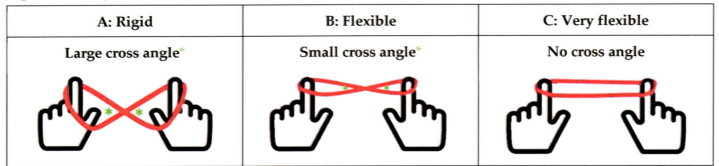

14 · The Easier Way to Knit

Using beads to track structure

Visualizing the structure of double knit fabric with a two-stitch wide chain is another way to learn about how double knit stitches are formed. A knitted chain, in addition to a beautiful accessory, enables stitches to be viewed from multiple angles without being crowded by adjacent stitches. The beaded stitches in Figure 28 help track the looping process by showing how a bead moves around the peg. In this beading method, beads are strung onto the ribbon before knitting. Instructions for knitting a beaded chain are summarized below. Note: Another method for adding beads is explained in the section on **Knitting with beads** (See page 39).

Figure 28: Loop tracking with a bead.

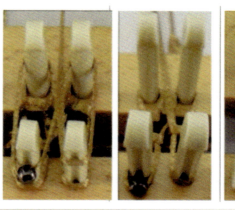

1. After casting on, add a bead.
2. After knitting off the loop under the bead.
3. After knitting off beaded loop.

Now, try loop tracking with a bead!

Materials	Instructions
1. Double rake loom 2. (2) 1 cm washers 3. 10 m of 2 mm ribbon 4. (2-8) round beads (3-8 mm) with 2 mm or larger holes	1. Bead preparation: Add two to eight beads to the ribbon before casting onto the loom. 2. Casting on: Weave one row of stockinette stitch around two pegs and add an anchor yarn. 3. Chain: Knit two rows of the stockinette stitch, position a bead on the middle of a peg, and repeat the process on the adjacent and the opposite pegs.

Exploring stitch modifications

Figure 29: Loom knit necklace.

Exploring the effects of stitch modifications is another way to visualize how the double rake loom works. This section illustrates modifications to the twisted stockinette stitch, such as the necklace in Figure 29. The twisted stockinette stitch was selected for this exercise because beads lie on the outside of the chain, unlike the stockinette stitch where the beads are less visible. The looping diagram for a two-peg twisted stockinette stitch is illustrated in Figure 30.

Figure 30: Looping diagram for the twisted stockinette stitch.

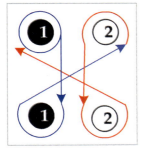

Wrap sequence: After attaching the yarn to peg 1 (BR) with a slip knot, bring the ribbon straight down and clockwise around peg 1 (FR) and up to the right side of peg 2 (BR). The return wrap is illustrated in red and mirrors the forward wrap. After completing the first wrap sequence, add an anchor yarn and continue knitting.

Double knit fabrics · 15

Table 1 illustrates various two-peg wide chains knitted with the twisted stockinette stitch. Each chain represents a modification to the standard twisted stockinette stitch and includes a photo of a 4-inch chain and a summary of the effect of the modification. The modifications include 1) adding a bead to every other stitch, 2) double looping each peg, 3) using two strands of ribbon, 4) weaving two forward and return wraps per stitch, 5) and looping every third peg, instead of every other peg.

Table 1: A comparison of modifications to the twisted stockinette stitch chain on the double knitting rake.

Modification	Photo	Effect / Detail
None		• Baseline standard
Add beads		• Decorative
Double looping pegs		• Adds a decorative raised loop knot
Two strands of ribbon		• Decreases gauge • Uses two strands of ribbon
Two forward and return wraps per stitch		• Flattens chain and increases gauge • Uses one ball of ribbon • Slower than knitting with two yarns
Looping every third peg		• Decreases gauge and elasticity

Gauge

Gauge is a measure of stitch density estimated by knitting a swatch and counting the number of stitches and rows per centimeter or per inch. (Note: This book uses metric measurements.) Figure 31 shows how these measures are used to determine how many pegs to wrap to knit (fabric width) and how many rows

Figure 31: The relationship between gauge and calculating how many pegs to wrap and rows to knit.

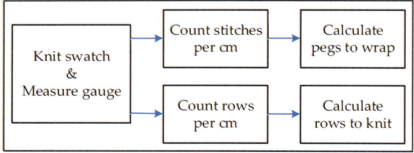

Figure 32: Gauge by weight.

Weight	Yardage 50 g	Stitches 10 cm
Lace	300 - 440	33 - 40
Super fine	200 - 300	27 - 35
Fine	180 - 200	23 - 26
Light	150 - 180	21 - 24
Medium	100 - 150	16 - 20
Bulky	50 - 100	12 - 15
Super bulky	<50	6 - 11

to knit (fabric length). Many factors affect gauge; these include yarn weight (See Figure 32 for gauge classification by yarn weight), stitch type, the distance between the rakes, the distance between pegs, the width of the pegs, the number of times a peg is wrapped, and the knitting tension. While each variable affects gauge, the distance between the rakes is especially important to double rake loom knitting because it is the only factor associated with the loom that can be varied to adjust gauge. The closer the rakes are to each other, the shorter the stitches and the larger the

16 · The Easier Way to Knit

gauge (more rows per cm); in contrast, rakes that are farther apart form longer stitches with a smaller gauge (fewer rows per cm). This relationship is summarized in Figure 33.

In addition, the effect of peg width and rake distance on gauge are illustrated in Figure 34. The three swatches in Figure 34 are knit using two different looms. Swatch 1 is knit on a Noble Knitter™ using rakes that are spaced 0.5 cm apart, and swatches 2 and 3 are knit on an 18" Knitting Board™ loom with rakes that are spaced 0.5 cm and 1.0 cm apart respectively. The Noble Knitter™, however, has narrower pegs that are spaced farther apart than the pegs on a Knitting Board™ loom. Swatches 1 and 2 illustrate that narrower pegs produce smaller stitches (more stitches per cm) and, therefore, a larger gauge (1.8 stitches/cm and 2.5 rows/cm). Swatches 2 and 3 illustrate that closer rakes form shorter stitches (1.5 rows/cm vs. 0.8 rows/cm). Not surprisingly, both swatches, which were knit on the same type of loom, have a nearly identical number of stitches per cm (1.1 stitch/cm vs. 1.0 stitch/cm).

Figure 33: Relationship between rake distance and gauge.

	Space between rakes	
	Narrow	Wide
Gauge	• Shorter stitches • More rows per cm • Larger gauge	• Longer stitches • Fewer rows per cm • Smaller gauge

Figure 34: Three stockinette brioche swatches knit with different gauges.

Swatch 1		Swatch 2		Swatch 3	
Gauge: Stitches/cm: 1.8 stitch /cm		Gauge: Stitches/cm: 1.1 stitch /cm		Gauge: Stitches/cm: 1.0 stitch /cm	
Rows/cm: 2.5 rows/cm		Rows/cm: 1.5 rows/cm		Rows/cm: 0.8 rows/cm	
Loom: 50 peg Noble Knitter™		Loom: 18" Knitting Board™		Loom: 18" Knitting Board™	
Distance between pegs	0.8 cm	Distance between pegs	0.5 cm	Distance between pegs	0.5 cm
Peg width	0.2 cm	Peg width	0.4 cm	Peg width	0.4 cm
Spacer width	0.5 cm	Spacer width	0.5 cm	Spacer width	1.0 cm
Yarn: Malabrigo™ worsted 210 yards/100g					

How many pegs to wrap?

The number of **pegs to wrap** equals the desired fabric width multiplied by the stitch density (the number of stitches per centimeter). The latter is estimated by knitting a swatch and dividing the number of stitches in row by its width. Figure 35 summarizes this relationship and Figure 36 shows sample calculations. Although the formulas look complicated, they only use addition, subtraction, multiplication, and division and they can be automatically calculated at www.rakeknitting.com using either centimeters or inches.

Figure 35: Number of pegs to wrap.

Number of pegs to wrap = Fabric width × Stitch density (From swatch)

Figure 36: Intermediary steps and examples for calculating the number of pegs to wrap (stitches to knit).

Measure	Formula	Example
Stitch density	$\dfrac{\text{No. of stitches}}{\text{Width}} \rightarrow \dfrac{\text{No. of stitches}}{1\text{ cm}}$	What is the stitch density of a 20-stitch swatch that is 16.0 cm wide? 20 stitches/16.0 cm → 1.25 stitches/1.0 cm
Pegs to wrap	$\left(\dfrac{\text{Fabric}}{\text{width}}\right)\left(\dfrac{\text{No. of stitches}}{1\text{ cm}}\right)$	How many pegs are needed to knit a 30.0 cm wide fabric if 1 cm equals 1.25 stitches? Pegs = $\left(\dfrac{\text{Fabric}}{\text{width}}\right)\left(\dfrac{\text{No. of stitches}}{1\text{ cm}}\right)$ = (30cm)$\left(\dfrac{1.25 \text{ stitches}}{\text{cm}}\right)$ = 37.5 stitches → round up to 38 pegs

How many rows to knit?

The number of **rows to knit** equals the fabric length multiplied by the row density (the number of rows per centimeter). The latter is estimated by knitting a swatch and dividing the number of rows by its length. Figure 37 summarizes this relationship and Figure 38 provides sample calculations.

Figure 37: Number of rows to knit.

Number of rows to knit = Fabric length × Row density (From swatch)

Figure 38: Intermediary steps and examples for calculating the number of rows to knit.

Measure	Formula	Example
Row density	$\dfrac{\text{No. of rows}}{\text{length}} \rightarrow \dfrac{\text{No. of rows}}{1\text{ cm}}$	What is the row density of a 20-row swatch that is 14 cm long? 20 rows/14 cm → 1.43 rows/1.0 cm
Rows to knit	$\left(\dfrac{\text{Fabric}}{\text{length}}\right)\left(\dfrac{\text{No. of rows}}{1\text{ cm}}\right) + 2$	If 1 cm equals 1.43 rows, how many rows are needed to knit an 80-cm fabric? Rows = (80 cm) · $\left(\dfrac{1.43 \text{ rows}}{\text{cm}}\right)$ + 1 cast-on row + 1 cast-off row = 114.4 rows + 2 = 116.4 → round up to 117 rows

18 · The Easier Way to Knit

While these formulas are very helpful, they depend on knitting consistent rows. However, stitch length can vary slightly, depending on how strongly fabric is pulled between the rakes. Pulling fabric strongly creates slightly longer stitches. Therefore, it is important to measure your fabric (See Figure 39), especially when seaming two fabrics together.

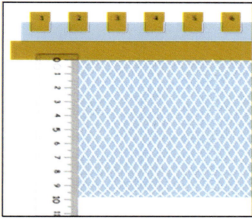

Figure 39: Measure fabric length.

Yarn estimator

The yarn needed for a project is estimated by the number of stitches in the project and by how much yarn is used in each stitch. The number of stitches is approximated by the number of stitches in a row multiplied by the number of rows. This relationship is summarized in Figure 40. Note that two additional rows are added to the formula, one row for casting on and one row for bind off. To calculate how many balls of yarn are needed, divide the yarn estimate by the length of a ball of yarn.

Figure 40: Yarn calculator.

$$\text{Yarn} = \begin{vmatrix} \text{Number of} \\ \text{pegs to wrap} \end{vmatrix} \times \begin{vmatrix} \text{Number of} \\ \text{rows to knit} \end{vmatrix} \times \begin{vmatrix} \text{Yarn to knit} \\ \text{one stitch} \end{vmatrix}$$

Yarn = (Number of stitches)(Yarn in a stitch)
     = (Stitches in a row)(Rows + 2)(Yarn in a stitch)

$$\text{Balls of yarn} = (\text{Yarn}) \left(\frac{1 \text{ Ball}}{\text{Yarn in one ball}}\right)$$

The amount of yarn needed to knit one double knit stitch depends on the same factors that affect gauge, such as the distance between the rakes, the size of the pegs, the distance between the pegs, yarn elasticity, and knitting tension. While these variables are important, the distance between the rakes is crucial for double rake loom knitting, because it is the only adjustable variable on the loom that affects gauge. Figure 41 illustrates the relationship between three different rake distances and the yarn needed to knit one double knit stockinette stitch. The corresponding yarn estimates, which were knit on an 18" Knitting Board™ loom, range from 5.7 to 6.7 cm per stitch. Figure 42 shows how to use these stitch estimates to calculate how much yarn is needed to knit a scarf that is 120 rows long and 30 stitches wide using a medium weight yarn with 182 meters of yarn per ball on a Knitting Board™ loom with rakes that are spaced 1 cm apart.

Figure 41: Yarn estimates for one double knit stockinette stitch on an 18" Knitting Board™ loom.

Distance between rakes (cm)	0.5	1.0	1.5
Yarn per stitch (cm)	5.7	6.0	6.7

Figure 42: Sample calculation for the number of balls of yarn needed to knit a scarf.

$$\text{Balls of yarn} = \boxed{\text{Yarn}} \times \boxed{\frac{1 \text{ Ball of yarn}}{\text{Yarn in 1 ball}}}$$

Balls of yarn = (Yarn needed for 1 stitch)$\left(\frac{\text{Stitches}}{\text{Row}}\right)$(Rows + 2)$\left(\frac{1 \text{ Ball}}{\text{Yarn in meters}}\right)\left(\frac{1 \text{ meter}}{100 \text{ cm}}\right)$

$= \left(\frac{6.0 \text{ cm}}{\text{Stitch}}\right)\left(\frac{30 \text{ stitches}}{\text{Row}}\right)(120 + 2 \text{ rows})\left(\frac{1 \text{ Balls}}{182 \text{m}}\right)\left(\frac{1 \text{ m}}{100 \text{ cm}}\right) = 1.21 \text{ balls} \rightarrow$ Round up to 2 balls

Double knit fabrics · 19

The equations used to customize fit and to estimate yarn are shown in Figure 43. Note that the white boxes are measured values and the colored boxes contain calculated values.

Figure 43: Yarn calculator.

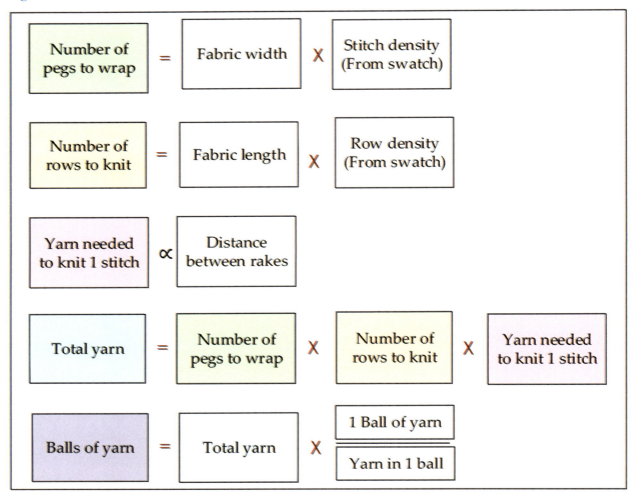

*White boxes contain measured values and colored boxed contain calculated values.

Use the knitting calculator at
www.rakeknitting.com
for all formulas in the book!

Knitting charts

Traditional knitting charts are a convenient tool for representing single knit fabrics; however, they are not well suited for double rake loom knitting because they neither specify whether instructions apply to the front or to the back rake nor do they specify crosses between the rakes. To address this, I developed a knitting chart system for double rake looms that includes rake specific instructions that can represent loop and stitch crosses on both the same rake and between rakes.

Knitoglyphics

Knitoglyphics (knitting symbols and abbreviations) for double rake knitting charts are summarized in Figure 44. The knitoglyphs include symbols for looping pegs and for adding stitches and crosses. The stockinette stitch is the default stitch in all knitting charts unless another stitch is specified. The wide rib cable© is an example of a stitch that is not stockinette based. Figure 52 explains how to interpret the knitting chart for the wide rib cable©, which is knit using the wide rib stitch.

Loops that are wrapped around a peg but are not knit off, such as cast-on or **tucked loops** (stitches with multiple loops), are symbolized by an open circle (O). Stitches, loops that are knit off, are symbolized with a solid circle (●), a bullseye (◎), or the letter K. A ● indicates that a loop is wrapped around a peg, and all bottom loop(s) are knit over the top loop. A numbered circle indicates the number of times a peg is looped. For example, 2● indicates that a peg is looped twice, and all bottom loop(s) are knit over the top loop. A bullseye (◎) indicates that the bottom loop is knit over the top two loops. The letter K also indicates that a loop needs to be knit off. It is used when the preceding step doesn't add a stitch, for example, after a cross or a bead.

Figure 44: Knitoglyphics for double rake knitting.

Looping and stitching symbols	
o	Loop peg but do not knit off.
●	Loop peg and knit off bottom loops.
2●	Loop peg twice and knit off bottom loop(s) over the top two loops.
⌐2●⌐	Undo the double loops on the BR and divide the excess yarn between the adjacent loops .
⸌2●⸜	Undo the double loops on the BR and divide the excess yarn between the catty-corner loops on the FR.
⸜2●⸍	Undo the double loops on the FR and divide the excess yarn between the catty-corner loops on the BR.
◎	Loop bottom loop over top two loops and knit off.
K	Knit off.
⑧	Replace a stockinette stitch with two figure 8 stitches.

Crosses		Abbreviations	
→	Right loop cross	FR	Front rake
←	Left loop cross	BR	Back rake
↑	Back loop cross	B	Add a bead
↓	Front loop cross	R	Reverse loop order
∨	Front stitch cross		
∧	Back stitch cross		

Loop crosses are represented with arrows that point in the direction of the cross. Similarly, stitch crosses are represented with a caret followed by an arrow that points in the direction of the cross (see pages 23-26 for a more complete discussion of loop and stitch crosses).

Interpreting knitting charts

Knitting charts for double rake looms are divided into three sections, a **preparatory section** (a.k.a. **prep**), a **repeat section** and an optional **end section**, which is only required for stitches that have a unique end, such as the last cross on a cable. Figure 45 illustrates a sample layout for a knitting chart. The preparatory section includes a cast-on row and may also include additional rows of stitches and/or crosses. Note: If the cast-on row uses a different stitch than subsequent rows, it will be specified in the stitch's instructions. The repeat section specifies the minimum number of rows that form a unit pattern. Each section has row specific instructions, which are either applied to one or both rakes. Instructions that are only applied to one rake are specified by a number followed by FR or BR. For example, 1 FR refers to row 1 on the FR and 1 BR refers to row 1 on the BR. Similarly, instructions that are applied to both rakes are labelled with a number without specifying a rake.

Figure 45: Knitting chart template.

Section	Instructions	Row
Repeat		
Prep		
	Peg Number	

Figure 46 shows the knitting chart for a stockinette brioche, an elastic, three-dimensional stitch. As the name suggests, stockinette brioche is a stockinette based stitch. The preparatory section includes a one-row stockinette cast-on, and the repeat section includes two rows of stockinette per repeating unit. The first row of the repeat section has rake specific instructions. On the FR (1 FR), the open circles indicate to weave the yarn around the pegs, and on the BR (1 BR), the closed circles indicate to weave the yarn around the pegs and to knit off the bottom loop(s) over the top loop. After completing row 1, the FR will have two loops on each peg, and the BR will have one loop on each peg. The knitting instructions for row 2 are not rake specific; therefore, looping the pegs and knitting off the bottom loop(s) over the top loop applies to both rakes. Note: Although the instructions for row 2 are not rake specific, the loops are knit slightly differently on each rake; this is because the BR has two loops on each peg, and the FR has three loops on each peg.

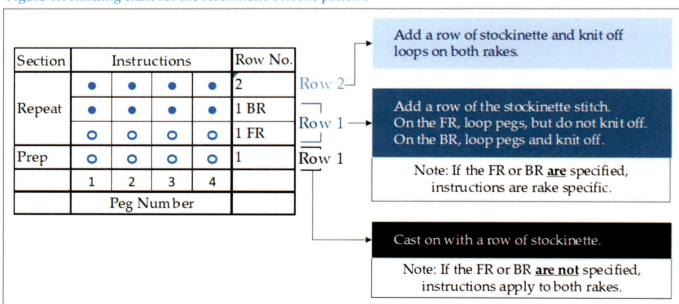

Figure 46: Knitting chart for the stockinette brioche pattern.

Crosses

Loop crosses

Cables are loops that are crossed over other loops. In traditional needle knitting, raised cables are knit next to receding purl stitches. This can be accomplished with rake loom knitting by reversing the order of the loops on a peg and knitting-off. However, I prefer forming cables using three other methods. Swatches for these three methods are illustrated in Figure 47. The first method creates flat cross stitches, such as the **right crosses** (a.k.a. right twists) using the stockinette stitch. The second method uses the cable rib stitch to create four stitch wide cables, separated by recessed, elastic slip stitches. Instructions for knitting the cable rib stitch are summarized on page 58. The third method creates three-dimensional crosses on a stockinette brioche fabric, a highly textured, elastic fabric knit with tucked stitches. Knitting instructions for right crosses on stockinette brioche are summarized on page 63.

Figure 47: Examples of three types of crosses on double knit fabric.

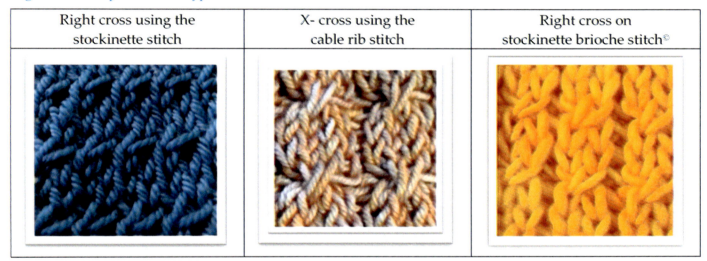

A right cross is a cross where the first loop (the left loop) is moved to the right, and then the right loop is moved to the left. Instructions for a single right cross are summarized in Figure 48. To create a right cross, 1) lift two adjacent loops off their pegs, 2) move the left loop to the right, and then 3) move the right loop to the left peg.

Figure 48: Instructions for a right cross.

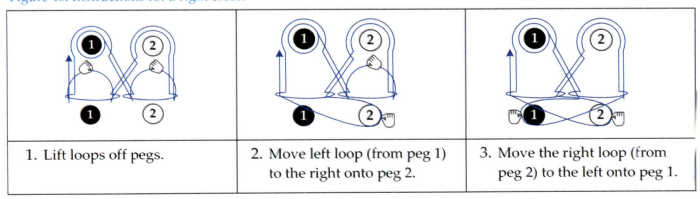

Knitting charts · 23

Notation for a right cross is illustrated in Figure 49 and Figure 50. This notation uses arrows to indicate the direction of the cross. Right and left arrows (→, ←) indicate loop transfers on the same rake. Up arrows (↖, ↗, ↑,) indicate **loop transfers** that create **elongated slip stitches** by moving a loop from the FR to the BR; similarly, down arrows (↙, ↘, ↓) indicate loop transfers that create elongated slip stitches by moving a loop from the BR to the FR. The superscript at the tail of the arrow indicates which loop is crossed first, second, third, etc., and the number after the arrow's point indicates the loop's new location. Figure 49 explains the notation; for example, the ^{1}→6 above peg 4 indicates that the loop on the fourth peg is moved first and should be placed on the sixth peg.

Figure 50 illustrates a sample knitting chart with multiple right crosses. Note: If a peg is moved to an adjacent loop, then the loop's new location is omitted. In addition, if the order of the move is not specified, then the order the loop transfers is not essential for the pattern, and loops can be moved from either right to left or left to right. For reference, Figure 54 summarizes cross notations for the double rake loom. However, their uses are explained in subsequent chapters when the notation is used.

Stitch crosses

Stitch crosses are similar to loop crosses, except stitch crosses move part of a stitch, instead of a loop, to a neighboring peg. The most common stitch crosses are to the opposite peg or to a catty-corner peg. Figure 51 shows a stitch cross from peg 1 on the BR to the opposite peg on the FR. A stitch cross from a peg on the BR to the opposite peg on the FR is symbolized with a down caret, "∨" and an arrow indicates its new location. For example, a right catty-corner stitch cross from the BR to the FR is symbolized by a down caret, ∨↘. Similarly, a right catty-corner stitch cross from the FR to the BR is symbolized by an up caret, ∧↗.

Knitting charts with crosses

Figure 52 explains how to interpret the knitting chart for the wide rib cable stitch©, an original stitch that applies the wide rib stitch (illustrated in Figure 53) to the knitting chart for the wide rib cable stitch©. Knitting directions are also detailed on pages 52-53.

The preparatory (prep) section in Figure 52 includes one row. Row 1, as always, represents the cast-on row. Note that although a cast-on stitch is not specified in the chart, it would be specified in a pattern, e.g., cast on with one rotation of twisted knit stitch.

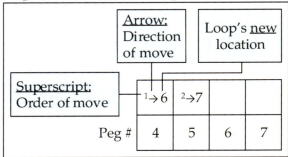

Figure 49: Notation for a right cross.

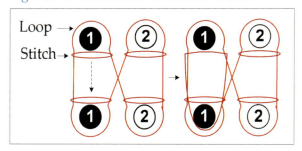

Figure 50: Knitting chart for right crosses.

Figure 51: Instructions for a stitch cross.

Figure 52: Knitting chart for the wide rib cable stitch and interpretation of the repeat section.

End	•	•	•	•	•	•	•	•	1
		•	•	•	•	•	•	•	•	3 BR
		•	•	o	•	•	o	•	•	3 FR
				K			K			2 BR
Repeat			↑			↑			2 FR
	•	•	•	•	•	•	•	•	2
		¹→4		2←²	¹→7		5←²		1 FR
	•	•	₂•	•	•	₂•	•	•	1 BR
	•	•	•	•	•	•	•	•	1 FR
Prep	o	o	o	o	o	o	o	o	1
	1	2	3	4	5	6	7	8	

Row 3:
- **Step 1 (3 FR & 3 BR):** Add a row of the wide rib stitch and knit off loop pairs. (On the FR, every third peg only has one loop and therefore, cannot be knit off.)

Row 2:
- **Step 3 (2 BR):** Knit off the loop pairs formed by the elongated slip stitches on the BR.
- **Step 2 (2 FR):** Add elongated slip stitches by moving every third loop on the FR to the BR.
- **Step 1 (2):** Add a row of the wide rib stitch and knit off.

Row 1:
- **Step 2 (1 FR):** Add a row of crosses on the FR.
- **Step 1 (1 BF & 1 BR):** Add a row of the wide rib stitch and double wrap every third peg on the BR. Knit off the loop pairs. Unwrap the double looped pegs and divide the excess yarn between the catty corner pegs on the FR.

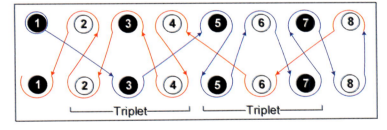

Figure 53: Looping diagram for the wide rib stitch.

The repeat section uses three rows of wide rib stitches to form a unit pattern.

Row 1 includes two steps. The first step has rake specific instructions. The filled circles represent adding a row of wide rib stitches. Note that every third peg on the BR has a ₂•. The 2 in front of the circle indicates that the peg is double wrapped and knit off. The arrows indicate that the excess yarn, formed by the double loop, is divided between the cattycorner pegs on the opposite rake. The second step adds a row of crosses on the FR that switch the first and third loop in each triplet.

Row 2 has three steps. The first step adds a row of wide rib stitches. The second step adds elongated slip stitches by moving every third loop on the FR (↑) to the opposite peg on BR. In the third step, the loop pairs formed by the elongated slip stitches on the BR are knit off (K).

Row 3, the last row in the repeat section, adds a row of wide rib stitches. Most cells in this row have closed circles. However, every third cell on the FR has an open circle. An open circle indicates that yarn is woven around a peg, but is not knit off. These cells have open circles, because the corresponding pegs are empty (their loops were used to form the elongated slip stitches in the previous step). These empty pegs can be looped, but require two loops to knit off.

The end section includes one row of wide rib stitches.

Knitting charts · 25

Figure 54: Summary of cross notation for the double rake loom.

Lateral crosses	Symbol	Explanation
Right cross		
Adjacent peg	$\rightarrow$	Move loop one peg to the right.
General*	$^n\!\rightarrow\! x$	The nth cross: Move loop to peg x on the same rake.
		• e.g., $^2\!\rightarrow\!3$: second cross moves the loop to the right to peg 3.
Left cross		
Adjacent peg	$\leftarrow$	Move loop one peg to the left.
General*	$x\!\leftarrow\!^n$	The nth cross: Move loop to peg x on the same rake.
		• e.g., $2\!\leftarrow\!^1$: first cross moves the loop to the left to peg 2.
Crosses to the opposite rake		
From BR to FR		
Directly across	$\downarrow$	Move loop from the BR to opposite peg on the FR.
Right catty-corner	$\searrow$	Move loop from the BR to right catty-corner peg on the FR.
Left catty-corner	$\swarrow$	Move loop from the BR to left catty-corner peg on the FR.
Right general*	$^n\!\searrow\! x$	The nth cross: Move loop to peg x on the opposite rake.
		• e.g., $^3\!\searrow\!2$: third cross moves the loop from the BR to peg 2 on the FR.
Left general*	$x\!\swarrow\!^n$	The nth cross: Move loop to peg x on the opposite rake.
		• e.g., $4\!\swarrow\!^3$: third cross moves the loop from the BR to peg 4 on the FR.
From FR to BR		
Directly across	$\uparrow$	Move loop from the FR to opposite peg on the BR.
Right catty-corner	$\nearrow$	Move loop from the FR to right catty-corner peg on the BR.
Left catty-corner	$\nwarrow$	Move loop from the FR to left catty-corner peg on the BR.
Right general*	$^n\!\nearrow\! x$	The nth cross: Move loop to peg x on the opposite rake.
		• e.g., $^1\!\nearrow\!2$: first cross moves the loop from the FR to peg 2 on the BR.
Left general*	$x\!\nwarrow\!^n$	The nth cross: Move loop to peg x on the opposite rake.
		• e.g., $4\!\nwarrow\!^3$: third cross moves the loop to peg 4 on the FR.

***Arrow indicates the direction of the move, superscript *n* identifies cross order (e.g., first, second, third, etc.), and x indicates the loop's or stitch's new location.**

Compound stitches

Compound stitches use multiple stitches. For example, the knitting chart for the crisscross stitch, which alternates between rows of the open braid stitch and the closed braid stitch, is shown in Figure 55. Symbols for stitches used in compound stitches are summarized in Figure 56.

Figure 55: Knitting chart for the crisscross stitch.

Repeat	C	C	2
	O	O	1
Prep	8	8	1
	1	2	

Figure 56: Stitch symbols.

Stitch	Symbol
Closed braid	C
Double figure 8	D8
Figure 8	8
Open braid	O
Slide	S
Stockinette	●

26 · The Easier Way to Knit

Knitting techniques

Before knitting patterns, some additional knitting skills need to be addressed. These include changing yarn strands, **shaping**, the process of increasing and decreasing fabric width, adding buttonholes, and seaming fabric together.

Changing yarns

Instructions for changing yarn strands are illustrated in Figure 57. To change yarns, connect the new yarn strand to the old yarn strand with an overhand knot, then lay the yarn ends on top of the slip stitches, and continue knitting.

Figure 57: Instructions for changing yarn on the double rake loom.

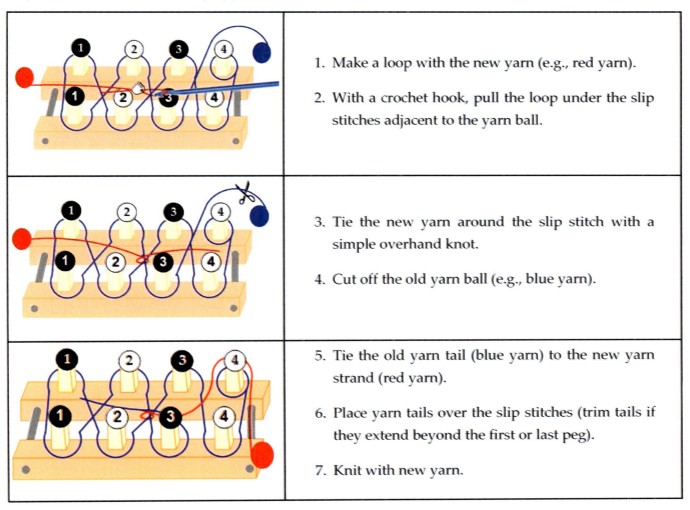

1. Make a loop with the new yarn (e.g., red yarn).
2. With a crochet hook, pull the loop under the slip stitches adjacent to the yarn ball.
3. Tie the new yarn around the slip stitch with a simple overhand knot.
4. Cut off the old yarn ball (e.g., blue yarn).
5. Tie the old yarn tail (blue yarn) to the new yarn strand (red yarn).
6. Place yarn tails over the slip stitches (trim tails if they extend beyond the first or last peg).
7. Knit with new yarn.

Shaping

Shaping is the process of increasing and decreasing fabric width to form a nonrectangular shape. Fabric width is increased with stitch crosses and decreased with loop crosses. Figure 58 describes how to add a stitch to increase the width of a fabric. A stitch can also be added to the middle of a fabric by moving loops to create an empty peg and then adding a stitch from an adjacent peg, using the techniques described in Figure 58.

Figure 58: Instructions for adding a stitch to a fabric's width.

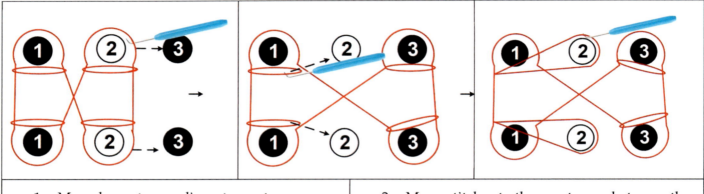

1. Move loops to an adjacent, empty peg.
   a. On the BR, move loop 2 to peg 3.
   b. On the FR, move loop 2 to peg 3.
2. Move stitches to the empty peg between the two loops.
   a. On the BR, move stitch 2 to peg 2.
   b. On the FR, move stitch 2 to peg 2.

Stitches are removed in a similar manner. Figure 59 illustrates how to remove a stitch to decrease a fabric's width. This is accomplished by moving a pair of loops onto an adjacent stitch and knitting off the loop pairs. A stitch in the middle of a piece of fabric can also be removed by moving a pair of loops onto an adjacent stitch and then moving each stitch to the right or to the left of the empty peg.

Figure 59: Instructions for removing a stitch in the middle of a fabric.

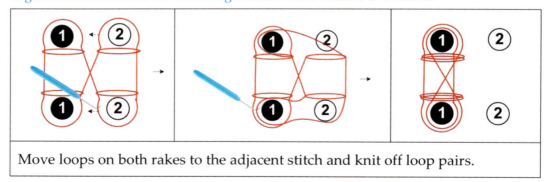

Move loops on both rakes to the adjacent stitch and knit off loop pairs.

Buttonholes

This section presents two methods for making a buttonhole. The first method forms a small buttonhole, such as the buttonhole in Figure 60, and the second method is used to create a large buttonhole or **keyhole** (a decorative circle in a garment) or to divide a fabric into two parts. Small buttonholes are formed with an **eyelet** (an empty stitch) that is reinforced at the top and the bottom of the eyelet. To reinforce the bottom of an eyelet, move the loops at the site of the eyelet to the catty-corner pegs as summarized in the annotated knitting chart in Figure 61 (steps 2 & 3). To complete the buttonhole, first, add a row of stockinette with two figure 8 stitches at the site of the buttonhole (as illustrated in Figure 62), and second, reinforce the top of the eyelet by switching the FR and BR loops formed by the figure 8 stitches.

Figure 60: A small reinforced buttonhole.

Figure 61: Directions for adding a small buttonhole.

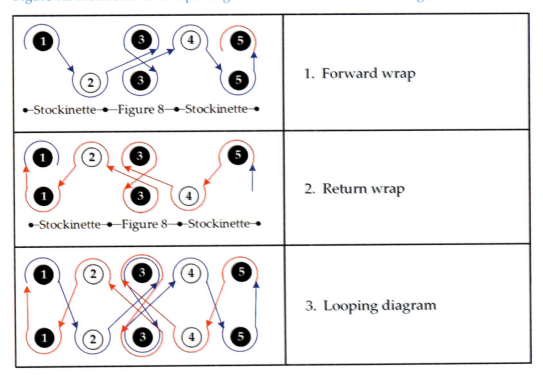

Figure 62: Instructions for replacing a stockinette stitch with two figure 8 stitches.

Knitting techniques · 29

Directions for adding a large buttonhole are summarized in Figure 63. This technique is also used to knit a keyhole or to divide a panel into two sections.

Figure 63: Directions for adding large buttonhole.

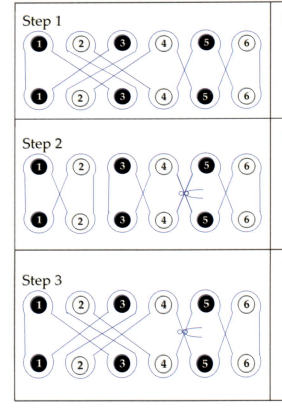

Step 1	**Reinforce the bottom of the buttonhole.** 1. Reinforce the bottom of the buttonhole with a right cross (e.g., between the second and third loops).
Step 2	**Divide the fabric into two sections.** 2. Divide the fabric by attaching a new yarn strand to the slip stitches on one side of the buttonhole (e.g., between pegs 4 and 5). 3. Knit one to five rows of stitches, depending on the size of the button and the gauge.
Step 3	**Reconnect fabric and reinforce the top of the buttonhole or keyhole.** 4. Knot one yarn strand (e.g., between the fourth and fifth loops). 5. Reinforce the top of the buttonhole with a right cross (e.g., between the second and third loops). 6. Continue knitting.

Seaming

Invisible seam

Figure 64 illustrates how to add an **invisible seam** to connect slip stitches on the vertical ends of two double knit fabrics. The result is a nearly invisible seam!

To hide the yarn strand, sew it between a column of stitches and add a knot, as illustrated in Figure 65.

Figure 65: Hide a yarn strand within a column of stitches.

Figure 64: An invisible seam on double knit fabric.

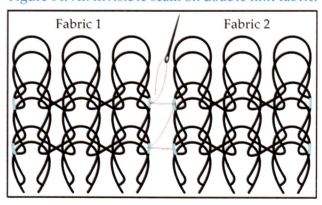

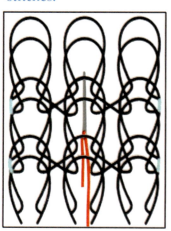

30 · The Easier Way to Knit

Color knitting

This chapter introduces the fundamentals of color theory, which can help you select color combinations and basic and advanced colored knitting techniques. The advanced techniques including intarsia, knitting with beads, simple brioche knitting, and stranded knitting. **Intarsia** is a knitting technique that uses areas of colors, such as geometric shapes, silhouettes, **tangrams** (figures constructed from thin wood blocks), or stained glass windows, to create designs. **Simple brioche** creates a fabric with different yarn on each side of the fabric. **Stranded knitting** uses slip stitches and **twisted slip stitches** to alternate or to replicate stitch colors and create two-colored patterns. This technique is also used to create multicolor patterns by knitting multiple rows with distinct two-colored patterns. In addition, to these color techniques, two color cables are discussed in the brioche knitting chapter.

Figure 66: Color harmonies.

Introduction to color theory

There are many ways to choose color combinations. Common selection methods include color combinations found in nature, existing patterns, available yarn, color theory, and internet based color swatches. The **color wheel**, illustrated in Figure 66, is a device for organizing primary, secondary, and tertiary colors and for selecting color harmonies. The **primary colors** include red, yellow, and blue. These colors are pure pigments that do not contain wavelengths of other colors and cannot be created by mixing other colors together. Combinations of red, yellow, and blue can create all secondary and tertiary colors. The **secondary colors,** green, orange, and purple, are created by mixing two primary colors. The remaining six colors on the color wheel are **tertiary colors**, which are mixtures of primary and secondary colors.

Two **color harmonies** include **complementary colors** and **analogous colors**. **Complementary colors** are colors that are opposite each other on the color wheel, such as red and green or yellow and purple. **Analogous or adjacent** colors are another common color harmony. Examples of analogous colors include red and fuchsia, red and orange, and blue and teal. **Triads** and **tetrads** are another way of selecting color harmonies. There are two triad color schemes, **true triads** and **split complementary** color schemes. True triads use every fourth color on the color wheel. **Split complementary** colors use a dominant base color and the two colors on either side of the complementary color. Two examples of split complementary colors are 1) red, light green, and teal and 2) violet, light green, and light orange. A **tetradic** color scheme is a color harmony that uses a rectangular pattern to select two complementary pairs, such as the red and green complement and its perpendicular complement, indigo and light orange.

Basic color techniques

The easiest way to incorporate color into knitted fabric is to knit with **variegated yarns**, yarns with multiple colors. There are many types of variegated yarns; common selections include tweeds with colored flecks, heathers, ombre, marled or twisted yarns, and self-striping yarns, such as Figure 67.

Figure 67: Self-striping yarn.

Horizontal stripes

Knit stripes by alternating rows of different yarns. Figure 68 is an example of a horizontally striped fabric that is knit with two different colored yarns. Note: If multiple rows of yarn are used, connect the new yarn strand to the old yarn strand with an overhand knot, lay the yarn ends on top of the slip stitches, and continue knitting (as illustrated in Figure 57). Knitting with two balls of yarn is straightforward if the unused yarn strand is hidden between two slip stitches. Tip: After knitting with the second yarn, tighten the stitch by pulling on the first yarn.

Figure 68: Alternating horizontal stripes.

Alternating vertical stripes

The alternating vertical stripes in Figure 69 are knitted with a stockinette stitch that uses two yarns and a twisted slip stitch at the end of each row, which forces each yarn strand to follow the previous wrap pattern. Figure 70 illustrates the difference between a slip stitch and a twisted slip stitch. (Note: The red and blue lines represent different colored yarn.) Add a twisted slip stitch by holding one ball of yarn in each hand and crossing the yarn twice. Figure 71 illustrates the looping diagram for alternating vertical stripes. The return wrap is identical to the forward wrap but in the opposite direction.

Figure 69: Alternating vertical stripes.

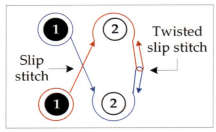

Figure 70: Comparison of a slip and a twisted knit stitch.

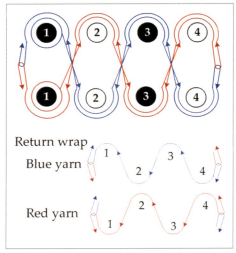

Figure 71: Looping diagram for alternating vertical stripes.

32 · The Easier Way to Knit

Creating slip stitches with a lazy Susan

Figure 72 illustrates how to form a twisted slip stitch on a lazy Susan. (Note that the red and blue lines represent yarn color.) Although a twisted slip stitch can be made without a lazy Susan, a lazy Susan expedites the process.

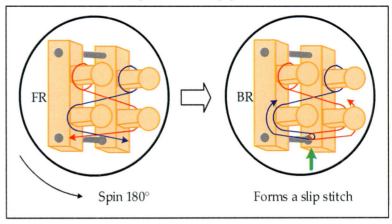

Figure 72: A twisted slip stitch at the end of a row forces the yarn to transverse the previous wrap pattern.

Forward wrap:

1. Place the loom on a lazy Susan with the FR facing left as illustrated in Figure 72.
2. With a slip knot, attach each yarn strand onto pegs on the opposite rakes.
3. Hide one yarn within a column of stitches (Figure 73) and bind off with the other yarn strand.
4. Weave the yarn around the pegs.
5. After looping the last pair of pegs, add a twisted slip stitch. (Weave a twisted slip stitch by holding one yarn strand in each hand close to the pegs and either turning the lazy Susan 180º clockwise or crossing the yarn twice.)

<u>The return wrap</u> is identical to the forward wrap but in the opposite direction.

Tips: Using a lazy Susan to add twisted slip stitches
1. Hold one strand of yarn in each hand.
2. Hold fingers close to the pegs.
3. To help prevent tangled yarn, place each yarn ball in a tall jar on either side of the lazy Susan.

Figure 73: Tips for knitting with two balls of yarn.

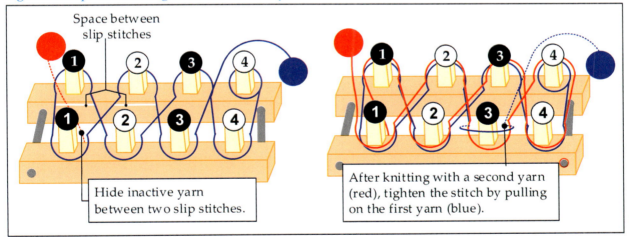

Color knitting • 33

Advanced color knitting techniques

Intarsia

Intarsia is a color knitting technique that creates designs with areas of color, like tangrams or stained glass windows. The results range from simple geometric designs and silhouettes, like the tulip in Figure 74, to complex designs. Note that the empty cells in Figure 74 represent stitches in a contrasting color. Sources for **charted patterns** (a pattern in a chart) include knitting and embroidery books, internet searches with the keywords knitting chart, cartoons, vector art, and public domain. Intarsia uses multiple, interconnect yarn strands to create seamless color changes. Figure 75 illustrates how to seamlessly interconnect the stitches. This technique is relatively straightforward. The only caveat is that the unused yarn strand needs to be hidden between two slip stitches, as illustrated in Figure 73, to prevent an uneven edge. Tip: After knitting with the second yarn, tighten the stitch by pulling on the first yarn.

Figure 74: Intarsia swatch and knitting chart.

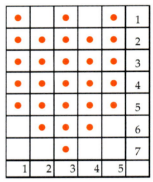

Figure 75: Instructions for interconnecting yarn strands.

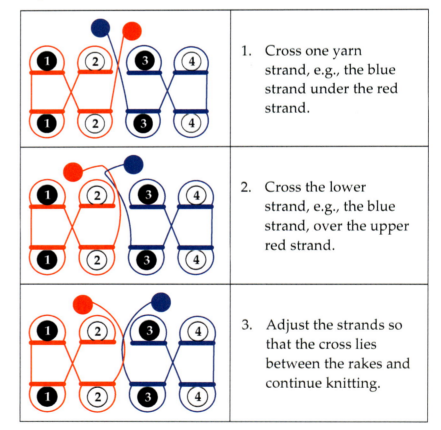

1. Cross one yarn strand, e.g., the blue strand under the red strand.

2. Cross the lower strand, e.g., the blue strand, over the upper red strand.

3. Adjust the strands so that the cross lies between the rakes and continue knitting.

34 · The Easier Way to Knit

Simple brioche

Simple brioche creates a stockinette fabric with different yarn on each side of the fabric. This is accomplished with twisted slip stitches that force each yarn strand to loop on the same rake, as the previous stitch. Figure 72 and Figure 76 illustrate how to add twisted slip stitches using a lazy Susan, and Figure 77 illustrates the forward and return wrap for the simple brioche stitch. (Note: The red and blue lines in these figures represent different color yarns.) Cast on with the simple brioche stitch or with the stockinette stitch.

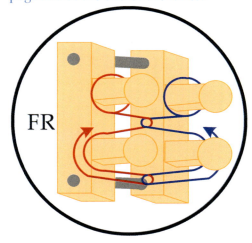

Figure 76: Twisted slip stitches between pegs and at the end of the rakes.

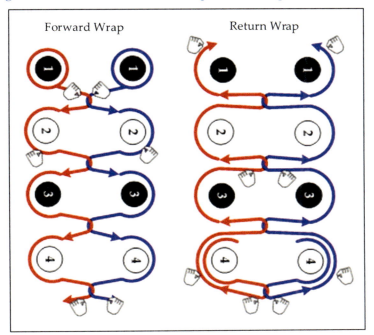

Figure 77: Forward and return wrap for the simple brioche stitch.

Color Knitting • 35

Stranded knitting

On a double rake loom, stranded knitting creates reversable color patterns using standard and twisted slip stitches. Figure 78 illustrates how alternating and repeating colors are created with standard and twisted slip stitches. Standard slip stitches force yarn strands to cross the rakes, which alternates colors on adjacent pegs; in contrast, twisted slip stitches force yarn strands to stay on the same rake and repeat the color on the previous peg. Instructions for creating twisted slip stitches are detailed in the previous section. The weaving technique for two-colored stranded knitting differs from standard double loom knitting. Usually, the double rake loom is held horizontally. However, in stranded knitting, the loom is held vertically (Figure 77) or lies vertically on a lazy Susan (Figure 79). Although the vertical orientation of the loom expedites two-colored knitting, it complicates the use of standard horizontal knitting charts. Fortunately, transposing the rows and columns alleviates this problem and is easily implemented with a spreadsheet program.

Figure 80 illustrates the vertical transposition of a standard horizontal knitting chart for a hound's tooth pattern. Transposing charts by hand is time consuming. However, Excel® or an open source spreadsheet, such as Apache OpenOffice™ or LibreOffice™, can easily transpose charts.

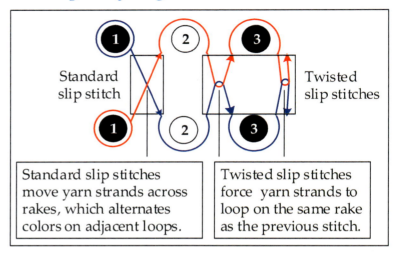

Figure 78: Use standard and twisted slip stitches to create alternating and repeating stitch colors.

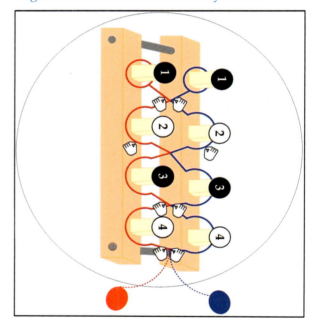

Figure 79: Vertical loom on a lazy Susan.

To transpose a chart in Excel:

1. Copy the chart.
2. Right click to paste the chart.
3. Select the paste option and left click on the transpose icon.

Figure 80: Horizontal swatch transposed vertically.

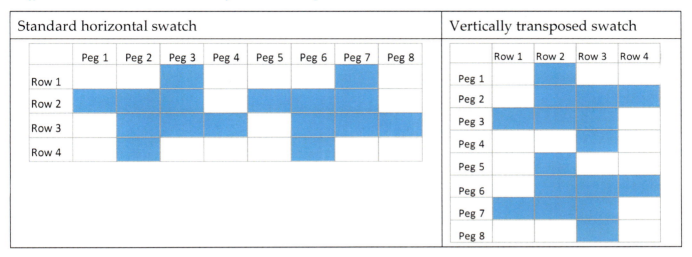

In addition to illustrating the pattern, a vertically transposed chart also needs to specify the knitting direction. On a vertically held loom, odd "rows" are now knitted down and even "rows" are knitted up. Figure 81 illustrates virtual swatches for a standard and a vertically transposed hound's tooth pattern, and a knitting chart for the vertically transposed swatch.

Figure 81: Virtual swatches and a knitting chart for a hound's tooth pattern.

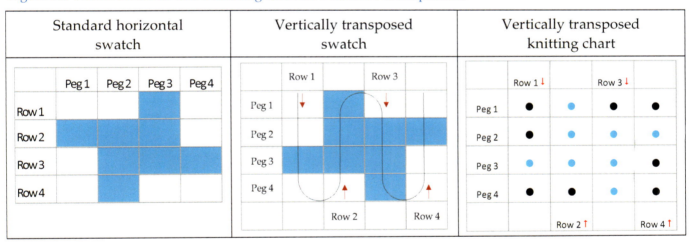

Color knitting • 37

Knitting with beads

Beads are a beautiful way to add color, highlights, and texture to knitted fabric. Beads can be used for borders, all-over designs, or as accents. Charted patterns for mosaic, stranded or lace knitting, and cross stitch are excellent sources for beading designs. Fortunately, adding beads to loom knitted fabric is relatively straightforward. However, the smaller the bead, the harder it is to thread. Size 6/0 **rocailles** (seed beads) with at least a 1.1 mm hole are perfect for worsted weight yarn.

Knitting diagrams with beads

There are two types of knitting charts with beads. Beaded pattern that are knit onto stockinette fabric can either use a "B" or a "●" to represent bead placement. In these diagrams, stockinette stitches without beads are symbolized with empty boxes. The beaded check pattern in Figure 82 is an example of an all-over beaded design. The second type of knitting diagram incorporates beads into crossed stitches, such as the Andaluz chain stitch with beads© (See Figure 95).

Figure 82: Knitting charts with beads.

Bead designs in stockinette: Beaded Check

1	2	3	4	5	6	7	8	
		●	●			●	●	8
		●	●			●	●	7
●	●			●	●			6
●	●			●	●			5
		●	●			●	●	4
		●	●			●	●	3
●	●			●	●			2
●	●			●	●			1

Bead designs in crossed stitches: Andaluz chain stitch with beads©

	1	2	3	4	5	6	
	●	●	●	●	●	●	3
		B			B		2 FR
Repeat	●	●	●	●	●	●	2 BR
	●	o	●	●	o	●	2 FR
		↑			↑		1 FR
Prep	●	●	●	●	●	●	2
	o	o	o	o	o	o	1

38 · The Easier Way to Knit

Figure 83 illustrates two methods for adding beads to fabric (See page 15 for a third method). These two methods both transfer a bead from a temporary holder onto a loop. However, I prefer the floss method.

Figure 83: Instructions for adding beads to loom knit fabric using floss or a crochet hook.

Beading a loop with floss	Beading a loop with a crochet hook
1. Knot floss around a bead. 2. Add a bead and push it towards the knot.	1. Thread a crochet hook through the bead.
3. Remove a loop from a peg and thread the floss through the loop.	2. Remove a loop from a peg.
4. Rethread the bead.	3. Hook loop tautly.
5. Tautly hold the needle and the beaded knot. 6. With the other hand, push the bead down the loop.	4. Push the bead down the loop.
7. Place a hook tool in the crux of the yarn loop. 8. Remove the floss. 9. Push the bead down.	5. Loop the yarn back around the peg. 6. Continue knitting.
10. Loop the yarn back around the peg. 11. Continue knitting.	

Color knitting • 39

Stitches

This book includes instructions for thirty-eight stitches, eleven of which are original. The original stitches include the Andaluz chain stitch with beads©, the large honeycomb tube stitch©, the narrow tube stitch©, the raised rib stitch©, right crosses on stockinette brioche©, the slipped tube stitch©, the small honeycomb tube stitch©, the spiral rib on stockinette brioche©, the wide rib cable with beads©, the wide rib cable©, and the x-cross rib cable©. Each stitch includes a swatch, a summary of its uses and decorative characteristics, knitting directions, and looping diagrams that summarize how to weave the stitch around the loom. Every forward wrap includes a repeat section that describes the pattern. If the first or last pegs are wrapped differently than the rest of the stitch, these are detailed in a begin and/or end section. Looping directions are also included for stitches with distinct return wraps.

If you are new to double rake loom knitting, I recommend experimenting with stitches in the *basic stitches section* or the twisted double rib stitch before knitting more complicated stitches.

40 · The Easier Way to Knit

Basic stitches

The basic stitches include the stockinette stitch and nine variations of the stockinette stitch.

Stockinette

The smooth, dense stockinette stitch is one of the most basic and versatile knitting stitches. In addition to its decorative uses, the stitch's distinct vertical lines facilitate casting onto the loom, shaping, and seaming. On the double knitting loom, the stockinette stitch is created by u-wrapping yarn around the outside of each catty-corner peg until the last peg. At the last peg, weave the yarn vertically across to the opposite rake and continue weaving the yarn until you reach the first peg. Figure 84 illustrates the looping diagram for the stockinette stitch. Cast on with the stockinette stitch.

Cast on: Add a slip knot onto peg 1 (BR), a row of stockinette, and an anchor.

Forward wrap: The forward wrap begins on the left side of each peg and alternates between clockwise loops on the BR and counterclockwise loops on the FR.

Repeat
1. Weave the yarn down to the left of peg 2 (FR) and counterclockwise around it.
2. Weave the yarn up to the left of peg 3 (BR) and clockwise around it.

End
1. Complete the forward wrap by weaving the yarn counterclockwise around peg 8 and straight across to the opposite peg.

Return wrap: The return wrap is identical to the forward wrap; however, empty pegs are looped in the opposite direction, which forces clockwise and counterclockwise loops on the FR and BRs respectively.

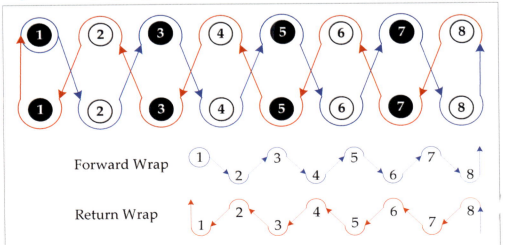

Figure 84: Looping diagram for the stockinette stitch.

Stitches · 41

Twisted stockinette stitch

The twisted stockinette stitch creates a dense fabric that is almost identical to the stockinette stitch. The only difference is that the stockinette stitch uses u-wraps and the twisted stockinette stitch uses e-wraps; e-wraps use more yarn than u-wraps and create a stretchier and thicker stitch than u-wraps. Cast on with the twisted stockinette stitch or a tight zigzag cast-on. Figure 85 illustrates the loop diagram for the twisted stockinette stitch.

Cast on: Add a slip knot onto peg 1 (BR), a row of twisted stockinette, and an anchor.

Forward wrap: Loops are wrapped clockwise on the FR and counterclockwise on the BR. All loops on the forward wrap begin on the right side of each peg.

Repeat
1. Weave the yarn down to the right of peg 2 (FR) and clockwise around it.
2. Weave the yarn up to the right of peg 3 (BR) and counterclockwise around it.

End
1. After wrapping the last peg in your sequence (e.g., peg 8 FR), bring the yarn straight up to the opposite peg (e.g., peg 8 BR).

Return wrap: The return wrap is identical to the forward wrap; however, empty pegs are looped in the opposite direction. Now, loops begin on the left side of each empty peg and are wrapped counterclockwise and clockwise on the FR and BR respectively.

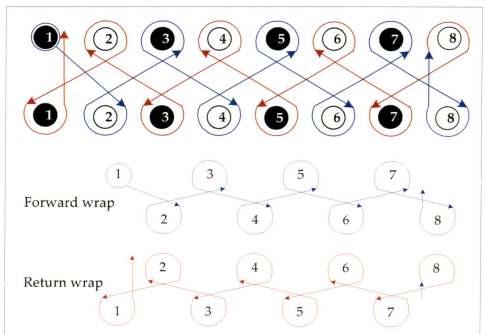

Figure 85: Looping diagram for the twisted stockinette stitch.

42 · The Easier Way to Knit

English stitch

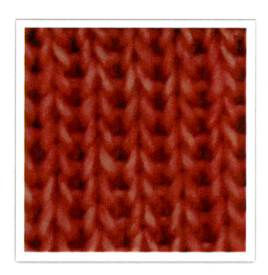

The English (a.k.a. waffle) stitch uses the stockinette's forward wrap for both its forward and return wraps, which creates a very soft fabric with exceptional elasticity. The waffle stitch is so stretchy that the width of this fabric is 40 percent narrower than the width of its wrap sequence on the loom. Cast on with the waffle stitch. Figure 86 illustrates the looping diagram for this stitch.

<u>Cast on</u>: Add a slip knot onto peg 1 (BR), a row of the English stitch, and an anchor.

<u>Forward wrap:</u> The forward wrap alternates between counterclockwise loops on the FR and clockwise loops on the BR.
Repeat
1. Weave the yarn down to the left of peg 2 (FR) and counterclockwise around it.
2. Weave the yarn up to the left of peg 3 (BR) and clockwise around it.

<u>Return wrap:</u> The return wrap loops around the same pegs as the forward loop. However, the directions of the loops are reversed.
Begin
1. Weave the yarn down to the right side of peg 6 (FR) and clockwise around it.
Repeat
1. Weave the yarn up to the right of peg 5 (BR) and counterclockwise around it.
2. Weave the yarn down to the right of peg 4 (FR) and clockwise around it.
End
1. Weave the yarn up to the left side of peg 1 (BR).

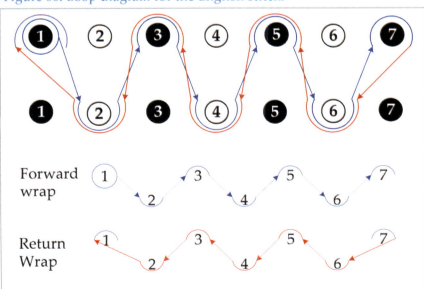

Figure 86: Loop diagram for the English stitch.

Stitches • 43

Single rib stitch

The single rib (a.k.a. slant-u or fashion) stitch is a stockinette variation with high crosswise elasticity and slight vertical elasticity. It is 30 percent narrower than the width of its wrap sequence on the loom. This stitch only requires one wrap to loop all the pegs. Cast on with the single rib stitch. The looping diagram for the single rib stitch is illustrated in Figure 87.

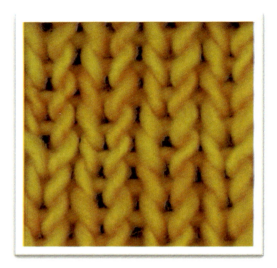

Cast on: Add a slip knot onto peg 1 (BR), a row of the single rib stitch, and an anchor.

Forward wrap: The forward wrap alternates between counterclockwise loops on the FR and clockwise loops on the BR. Loops begin on the left side of each peg.

Repeat
1. Weave the yarn down to left of peg 1 (FR) and counterclockwise around it.
2. Weave the yarn up to the left of peg 2 (BR) and clockwise around it.
3. Weave the yarn down to the left of peg 2 (FR) and counterclockwise it.

End
1. Weave the yarn straight up to the right of peg 8 (BR) and clockwise around it.

Return wrap: The return wrap is the same as the forward wrap but in the opposite direction, which forces counterclockwise loops on the BR and clockwise loops on the FR. However, the first and last pegs are wrapped differently.

Begin
1. Weave the yarn down to the right of peg 7 (FR) and counterclockwise around it.

End
1. Weave the yarn straight back and clockwise around peg 1 (BR).

Figure 87: Loop diagram for the single rib stitch.

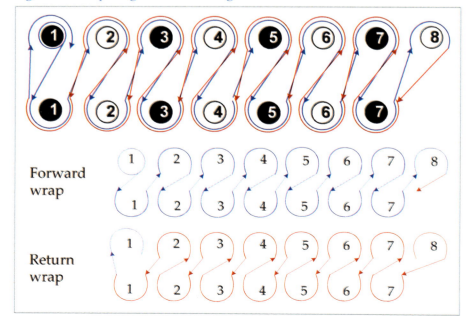

44 · The Easier Way to Knit

Zigzag stitch

The zigzag stitch is an elastic crosswise stitch with an angular plaited pattern. This stitch only requires one wrap to loop all the pegs in a loop sequence. Cast on with the zigzag stitch or the twisted knit stitch. The looping diagram for this stitch is illustrated in Figure 88.

Cast on: Add a slip knot to peg 1 (BR), a row of the zigzag stitch, and an anchor.

Forward wrap: The forward wrap begins on the left side of each peg and alternates between counterclockwise loops on the FR and clockwise loops on the BR.

Repeat
1. Weave the yarn down to the left of peg 1 (FR) and counterclockwise around it.
2. Weave the yarn up to the left of peg 2 (BR) and clockwise around it.
3. Weave the yarn down to the left of peg 2 (FR) and counterclockwise around it.

End
1. After looping the last peg in your sequence, weave the yarn straight up to the BR.

Return wrap: The return wrap loops the same pegs as the forward wrap but in the opposite direction. This creates counterclockwise loops on the BR and clockwise loops on the FR. All loops begin on the right side of the peg.

Figure 88: Looping diagram for the zigzag stitch.

Stitches • 45

Twisted knit stitch

The decorative and elastic twisted knit (a.k.a. twisted rib or double knit 8) stitch has very different patterns on each side of the fabric. This stitch is convenient for seaming, since it has two distinctive horizontal lines, which helps identify individual stitches during seaming. The

twisted knit stitch only requires one wrap to loop all the pegs in a row. Cast on using the forward wrap of the twisted knit stitch. The looping diagram for this stitch is illustrated in Figure 89.

Cast on: Add a slip knot to peg 1 (BR) and add a row of the twisted knit stitch.

Forward wrap: The forward wrap alternates between counterclockwise loops on the BR and clockwise loops on the FR.

Repeat
1. Weave the yarn down to the right of peg 1 (FR) and clockwise around it.
2. Weave the yarn up to right of peg 2 (BR) and counterclockwise around it.

End
1. Weave the yarn up to the right of the last peg (peg 8 BR) and counterclockwise around it.

Return wrap: The return wrap follows the same path as the forward wrap but in the opposite direction. To begin the return wrap, add a counterclockwise loop to peg 8 on the BR, weave the yarn down to the FR, and add a counterclockwise loop to the last peg on the BR. Weave the yarn to the left of peg 7 and clockwise around it and continue knitting.

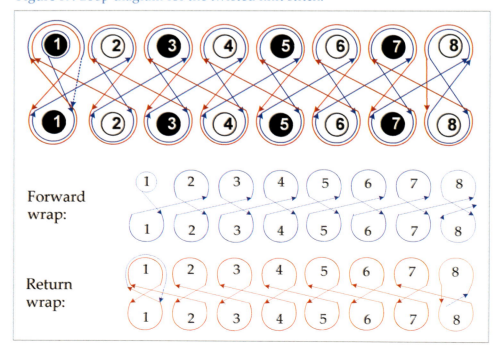

Figure 89: Loop diagram for the twisted knit stitch.

46 · The Easier Way to Knit

Little bee stitch

The little bee stitch is a stockinette variation that alternates between a fashion stitch on the BR and a twisted knit stitch on the FR. The alternating stitches produce long parallel slip stitches, which in turn creates a very soft, open, and elastic fabric. The e-wraps in this stitch are a little different than other e-wraps. Thus far, e-wraps either looped two vertical or two horizontal slip stitches. In contrast, the e-wraps in the little bee stitch are looped between vertical and horizontal slip stitches. Figure 90 illustrates the different types of e-wrap loops. Cast on with the stockinette stitch, the twisted knit stitch, the twisted double rib stitch, or the little bee stitch. Figure 91 illustrates the loop diagram for the little bee stitch.

Cast on: Add a slip knot to peg 1 (BR), a row of the little bee stitch, and an anchor.

Forward wrap: Pegs on both rakes are looped clockwise. Pegs on the BR are looped with u-wraps, like the fashion stitch, and pegs on the FR are looped with e-wraps, like the twisted knit stitch.

Repeat
1. Weave the yarn down to the right of peg 1 (FR) and clockwise around it.
2. Weave the yarn up to the left of peg 2 (BR) and clockwise around it.

End
1. Weave the yarn straight down to the opposite peg, loop the yarn clockwise around the peg, and knit off.

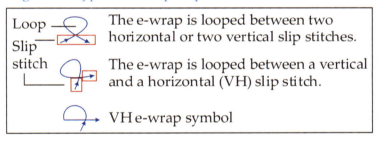

Figure 90. Types of e-wrap loops.

Return wrap: Pegs on the return wrap are looped clockwise with e-wraps on the BR and u-wraps on the FR.

Begin
1. Weave the yarn clockwise around peg 8 (FR).

Repeat
1. Weave the yarn straight across to the (BR) and loop the yarn clockwise around the peg.
2. Weave the yarn down to the right of peg 7 (FR) and clockwise around it.

End
1. Weave the yarn straight up to the opposite peg, loop the yarn clockwise around the peg and knit off.

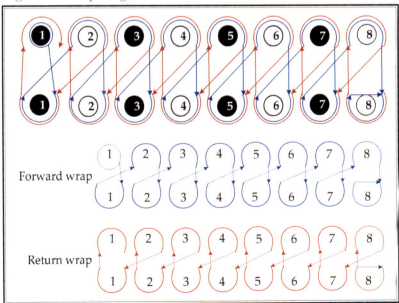

Figure 91: Loop diagram for the little bee stitch.

Stitches • 47

Rib stitches

Rib stitches are laterally contracting stitches that are used decoratively and for tight fitting boarders like cuffs and hems. This section presents several different types of rib stitches, including rib stitches with wide and narrow columns and low and high dimensionality. In addition, two stitches listed in the *basic stitches section*, the single rib and the twisted knit stitch, are rib stitches.

Raised rib stitch©

The raised rib stitch© is my favorite rib stitch. It is a very elastic, tightly knit stitch with raised ribs and recessed troughs. Knit the raised rib stitch by casting on with a twisted knit stitch and then knitting the loopy box stitch. The Raised rib stitch©, which loops around pairs of pegs, knits quickly because it takes less time to loop a pair of pegs than to loop individual pegs. The looping diagram for the loopy box stitch is illustrated in Figure 92.

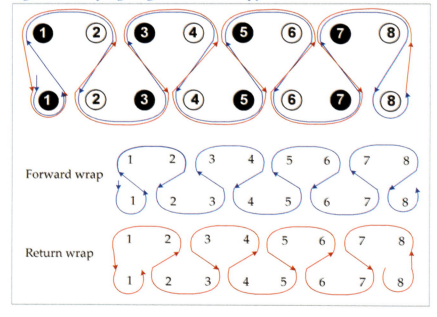

Figure 92: Looping diagram for the Loopy box & raised rib stitches.

Cast on: Add a slip knot onto peg 8 (FR) and add a row of the twisted knit stitch.

Forward wrap: The forward wrap alternates between clockwise loops on the BR and counterclockwise loops on the FR.

Repeat
1. Weave the yarn down to the left of peg 1 (FR) and counterclockwise around it.
2. Weave the yarn up to the right of pegs 1 and 2 (BR) and clockwise around it.
3. Weave the yarn down to the left of peg 2 (FR) and counterclockwise around pegs 2 and 3.

End
1. After weaving the yarn clockwise around pegs 7 and 8 (BR), weave the yarn down to the left of peg 8 (FR) and counterclockwise around it.

Return wrap: The return wrap is identical to the forward wrap, but the yarn is wrapped in the opposite direction. That forces counterclockwise loops on the BR and clockwise loops on the FR.

Twisted double rib stitch

The twisted double rib (a.k.a. box) stitch is one of the most versatile stitches. With alternating ridges and furrows, the twisted double rib stitch is decorative, elastic, and easy to knit. Unlike most stitches, the twisted double rib stitch only requires one wrap sequence to knit a row of stitches. Cast on with the twisted knit stitch or the twisted double rib stitch. Figure 93 illustrates the looping diagram for this stitch.

Cast on: Add a slip knot to peg 1 on the BR and knit a row of the twisted double rib stitch.

Forward wrap: Loops alternate between counterclockwise loops on the BR and clockwise loops on the FR. The first rotation of the forward wrap differs slightly from subsequent rotations; the difference is summarized in the looping diagram and in the text below.

Repeat
1. Weave the yarn down to the right of peg 1 (FR) and clockwise around it.
2. Weave the yarn horizontally to the right of peg 2 (FR) and clockwise around it.
3. Weave the yarn up to the right of peg 2 (BR) and counterclockwise around it.
4. Weave the yarn horizontally to the right of peg 3 (BR) and counterclockwise around it.

End (For the first row of the twisted double stitch)
1. After looping the last pair of pegs on the FR, weave the yarn up to the right and counterclockwise around the last peg on the BR.

End (For the subsequent rows of the twisted double stitch)
1. After looping the last pair of pegs on the FR, weave the yarn up to the right and counterclockwise around the last peg on the BR, knit off, and loop the peg again.

Return wrap: The return wrap is identical to the forward wrap. However, the return wrap loops pegs in the opposite direction. This creates clockwise loops on the BR and counterclockwise loops on the FR.

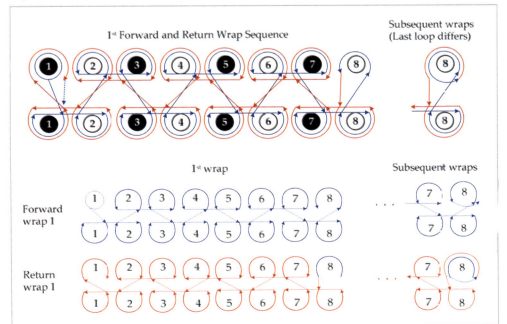

Figure 93: Looping diagram for the twisted double rib stitch.

Andaluz stitch

The Andaluz (a.k.a. alligator) stitch is a moderately elastic rib stitch that forms three-stitch wide puffy ridges separated by tight horizontal slip stitches. The Andaluz stitch requires multiples of three stitches and has very distinct forward and return wrap sequences. The forward wrap is straightforward, but the return wrap, which weaves both forward and backward, is complicated. Cast on with the stockinette stitch, the twisted knit stitch, or add a tight zigzag cast-on. Figure 94 illustrates the loop diagram for this stitch.

Cast on: Add a slip knot to peg 9 (BR), a row of stockinette, and an anchor.

Forward wrap: The forward wrap alternates between counterclockwise loops on the FR and clockwise loops on the BR.

Repeat
1. Weave the yarn down to the left of peg 2 (FR) and counterclockwise around it.
2. Weave the yarn up to the left of peg 4 (BR) and clockwise around it.

End: At the next to the last peg, weave the yarn up to the right of peg 9 (BR).

Return wrap: The return wrap follows a star-like pattern, which begins in the upper right corner. All pegs are looped clockwise, except for (BR) pegs that are multiples of three, which are looped counterclockwise.

Repeat
1. Weave the yarn counterclockwise around peg 9 (BR).
2. Weave the yarn down to the right of peg 7 (FR) and clockwise around it.
3. Weave the yarn up to the left of peg 8 (BR) and clockwise around it.
4. Weave the yarn down to the right of peg 9 (FR) and clockwise around it.
5. Weave the yarn up to the right of peg 6 and counterclockwise around.

End: Weave the yarn up to the left of peg 1 (BR).

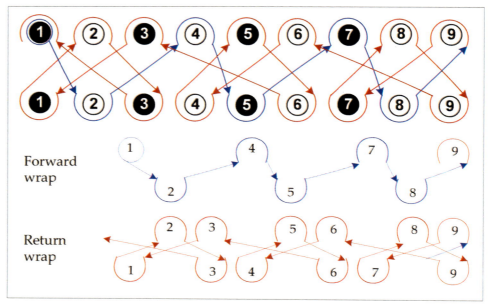

Figure 94: Loop diagram for the Andaluz stitch.

50 · The Easier Way to Knit

Andaluz chain stitch with beads©

The Andaluz chain stitch with beads© is a multistep decorative rib stitch that is knit using the Andaluz stitch (See Figure 94 for the looping diargram of the Andaluz stitch). Cast on with the Andaluz stitch, the figure 8 stitch, or a tight zigzag cast-on. The knitting chart for this stitch is summarized in Figure 95.

Knitting instructions

Preparatory section
1. Add a row of the Andaluz stitch and an anchor.

Repeat section
1. Add a row of the Andaluz stitch.
2. Add an elongated slipped stitch by moving the second loop in each Andaluz triplet to the opposite peg on the BR (e.g., loops on peg 2, 5, 8, etc.)
3. Add two rows of the Andaluz stitch and knit off bottom loop(s) over the top loop.
4. Add a bead to the middle loop in each triplet.

End section
1. Add a row of the Andaluz stitch and knit off.

Figure 95: Knitting chart for the Andaluz chain stitch with beads©.

End	•	•	•	•	•	•	•	•	1
			B			B			3 FR
	•	•	•	•	•	•	•	•	3
	•	•	•	•	•	•	•	•	2 BR
Repeat	•	•	O	•	•	O	•	•	2 FR
			↑			↑			1 FR
	•	•	•	•	•	•	•	•	1
Prep	O	O	O	O	O	O	O	O	1
	1	2	3	4	5	6	7	8	

Stitches • 51

Wide rib stitch

The wide rib stitch uses an asymmetrical wrap sequence to create an elastic fabric that alternates between three-stitch wide, slightly convex columns and narrow, elastic slip stitches on the front side of the fabric and a stockinette-like pattern on the back side of the fabric. The wide rib stitch requires multiples of three stitches plus two additional stitches (e.g., thirty-two stitches). Cast on with the stockinette stitch, the twisted knit stitch or the tight zigzag cast-on. Figure 96 illustrates the loop diagram for this stitch.

Cast on: Add a slip knot to peg 1 (BR) and a row of stockinette.

Forward wrap: The forward wrap alternates between clockwise loops on the BR and counterclockwise loops on the FR.

Repeat

1. Weave the yarn down to the left of peg 3 (FR) and counterclockwise around it.
2. Weave the yarn up to the left of peg 5 (BR) and clockwise around it.
3. Weave the yarn down to the left of peg 5 (FR) and counterclockwise around it.
4. Weave the yarn up to the left of peg 6 (BR) and clockwise around it.
5. Weave the yarn down to the left of peg 7 (FR) and counterclockwise around it.
6. Weave the yarn up to the left of peg 7 (BR) and clockwise around it.
7. Weave the yarn down to the left of peg 8 (FR) and counterclockwise around it.

End: Weave the yarn straight up to the right of peg 8 (BR).

Return wrap: The return wrap is identical to the forward wrap. However, the return wrap loops empty pegs in the opposite direction. This creates clockwise loops on the FR and counterclockwise loops on the BR.

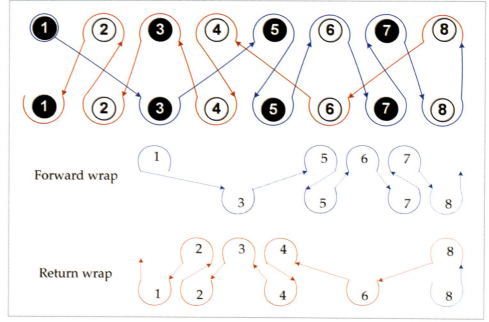

Figure 96: Looping diagram for the wide rib stitch.

52 · The Easier Way to Knit

Wide rib cable©

The wide rib cable© is a multistep stitch that applies the wide rib stitch to the wide rib cable pattern, which creates three-stitch-wide mock cables. The looping diagram for the wide rib cable stitch is illustrated in Figure 96. This stitch requires multiples of three stitches, plus two additional stitches for the first and last stitches, which are not crossed. Form a **one-three right cross** (a right-cross that switches the first and third loop in each wide rib triplet) on the FR and knit off loop pairs on the BR. Add a row of the wide rib stitch, add an elongated slip stitch from the FR to BR on every middle stitch in the triplet, and knit off loop pairs on the BR. Complete the stitch with two rows of the wide rib stitch. The knitting chart for this stitch is illustrated in Figure 97 and detailed in Figure 52.

Knitting instructions

Preparatory section (Rows 1-2)
1. Add a tight zigzag cast-on and an anchor;

Repeat section (Rows 1-3)
1. Add a row of the wide rib stitch, double wrap every third peg on the BR. After knitting off all the loop pairs, unwrap the double looped pegs and divide the excess yarn between the cattycorner loops on the opposite rake;
2. Form a one-three right cross (a right-cross that switches the first and third loop in each triplet) on the FR:
   a. Move the first loop in each triplet (e.g., loops 2, 5, etc.) to the third peg in each triplet (e.g., 4, 7, etc.).
   b. Move the third loop in each triplet to the first peg in the triplet.
3. Knit one row of the wide rib stitch and add an elongated slip stitch by moving the middle loop from each triplet on the FR (e.g., loops on peg 3, 6, etc.) to the opposite peg on the BR and knit off.
4. Knit a row of the wide rib stitch.

Figure 97: Knitting chart for the wide rib cable©.

Wide rib cable stitch with beads©

The wide rib cable stitch with beads© is a multistep stitch that applies the wide rib stitch, which is illustrated in Figure 96, to the knitting chart for the wide rib cable with beads in Figure 98. This stitch requires multiples of three stitches, plus two additional stitches for the first and last stitches. Add a row of the wide rib stitch, double looping every middle stitch in a wide rib triplet on the BR (e.g., pegs 3 and 6, etc.), and knit off loop pairs. Undo the double loops on the BR and divide the extra yarn between the catty-corner loops on the FR. Use the extra yarn to form a one-three right cross (a right-cross that switches the first and third loop in each triplet). Add a bead to the middle stitch in each triplet followed by an elongated slip stitch from the FR to BR. Complete the stitch by knitting two rows of the wide rib stitch.

Knitting instructions

Preparatory section (Rows 1-2)
1. Add a tight zigzag cast-on and an anchor.

Repeat section (Rows 1-3)
1. Loosely add a row of the wide rib stitch and double wrap the middle peg in each wide rib triplet on the BR (e.g., loops 3, 6). After knitting off the loop pairs, unwind the double wrapped middle pegs and divide the excess yarn to the catty-corner pegs on the FR (e.g., loops 2 and 4 and 5 and 7).
2. Form a one-three right cross (a right-cross that switches the first and third loop in each triplet) on the FR:
    a. On the FR, move the first loop in each triplet (e.g., loops 2, 5, etc.) to the third peg in each triplet (e.g., 4, 7, etc.).
    b. On the FR, move the third loop in each triplet to the first peg in the triplet.
    c. Add a bead to the middle loop in each triplet (e.g., loops 3, 6, etc.).
    d. Add an elongated slip stitch by moving the beaded loop (e.g., loops on pegs 3, 6, etc.) to the opposite peg.
3. Knit two rows of the wide rib stitch.

Figure 98: Knitting chart for the wide rib cable stitch with beads©.

54 · The Easier Way to Knit

Slipped tube stitch©

The slipped tube stitch© is a multistep, laterally elastic stockinette variation with distinct patterns on each side of the fabric. The front alternates between raised columns of stockinette stitches and recessed columns of elongated slip stitches, while the back of the fabric has a stockinette pattern. Knit this stitch on an odd number of pegs. The knitting chart for this stitch is illustrated in Figure 99.

Knitting instructions

Preparatory section (Row 1)
1. Add a row of stockinette and an anchor.
2. Add a second row of stockinette and knit off loop pairs.

Repeat section (Rows 1)
1. Add elongated slip stitches on even stitches:
   a. Move even loop on the FR to the opposite peg on the BR.
2. Add a row of stockinette and knit off bottom loop(s) over the top loop.

End section (Rows 1)
1. Add a row of stockinette and cast off.

Figure 99: Knitting chart for the slipped tube stitch©.

End	●	●	●	●	●	●	●	●	●	1
	●	●	●	●	●	●	●	●	●	1 BR
Repeat	●	o	●	o	●	o	●	o	●	1 FR
		↑		↑		↑		↑		FR
Prep	●	●	●	●	●	●	●	●	●	2
	o	o	o	o	o	o	o	o	o	1
	1	2	3	4	5	6	7	8	9	

Stitches • 55

Double rib stitch

The double rib (a.k.a. ribbing) stitch is a three-dimensional rib stitch with high elasticity. This stitch is also used to make cables (see cable rib stitches). Knit this stitch on an even number of pegs and cast on with the twisted knit stitch, the double rib stitch, or a tight zigzag cast-on. The looping diagram for this stitch is illustrated in Figure 100.

Cast on: Add a slip knot to peg 8 (BR), add a row of the twisted knit stitch, and an anchor.

Forward wrap: Pegs on the FR and BR are looped counterclockwise and clockwise respectively.

Begin
1. Weave the yarn clockwise around peg 1 (BR) and down to the left of peg 2 (FR).

Repeat
1. Weave the yarn counterclockwise around peg 2 (FR).
2. Weave the yarn up to the left of peg 2 (BR) and clockwise around it.
3. Weave the yarn down to the left of peg 4 (BR).

Return wrap: The return wrap follows the same path as the forward wrap. However, the return wrap loops empty pegs in the opposite direction. This forces counter-clockwise loops on the BR and clockwise loops on the FR.

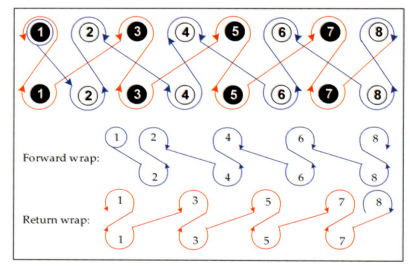

Figure 100: Loop diagram for the double rib stitch.

Double rib stitch variation

The double rib stitch variation in Figure 101 combines double rib stitches with stockinette stitches, which creates raised ribs or can be used to create raised cables (see Figure 102 and Figure 103) against a flat stockinette background.

Figure 101: Looping diagram for the double rib stitch variation.

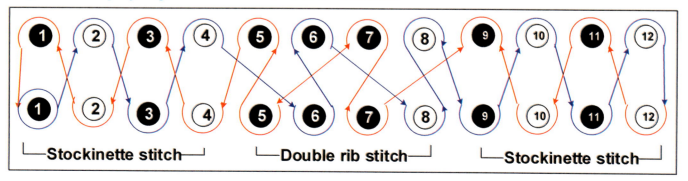

56 · The Easier Way to Knit

Cable rib stitch

The cable rib stitch is a modification of the double rib stitch that creates an elastic rib with four-stitch-wide cables, separated by recessed, elastic slip stitches. This fabric is 50 percent narrower than its wrap sequence. The cables are formed by switching pairs of crossed loops (loops with a cross angle) around an open pair of loops (loops without a cross angle). Figure 102 illustrates the crossing and looping crossing strategy for this cable. To form this cable, switch two adjacent crossed pair loops. For example, in Figure 102, switch the loops on pegs 2 and 3 with the loops on pegs 4 and 5. To switch the crossed pairs, first, pick up the loops that will be not visible (the loops that are moved last). Second, move the pair of loops that will be visible to the adjacent empty pegs. Lastly, move the second pair of loops to the adjacent empty pegs. Cast on with the double ribs stitch, twisted knit stitch, or a tight zigzag cast-on. The knitting chart for this multistep stitch is illustrated in Figure 103.

Knitting instructions

Preparatory section (Rows 1-2)
1. Add a tight zigzag cast-on.

Repeat section (Rows 1-4)
1. Add a four-loop cross:
   a. Lift off loops with superscripts 3 and 4.
   b. Move loops with the superscripts 1 and 2 to the pegs with the superscripts 3 and 4.
   c. Move loops with the superscripts 3 and 4 to the pegs with the superscripts 1 and 2.
2. Knit three to five rows of the double rib stitch.

End section (Row 1)
1. Add a four-loop cross (see 1a).
2. Add a row of the double rib stitch.

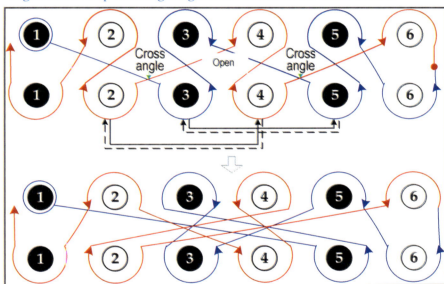

Figure 102: Loop crossing diagram for a double rib cable stitch.

Figure 103: Knitting chart cable rib stitch.

X-cross rib cable©

The x-cross rib cable© is a multistep stitch that uses the double rib stitch to create an x-cross rib stitch. An x-cross cable has two loop crosses: an inner loop cross followed by outer one. Figure 104 illustrates the difference between a standard cable and x-cross cable©. Cast on with the double ribs stitch, the twisted knit stitch or a tight zigzag cast-on. The knitting chart for this stitch is summarized in Figure 105.

Knitting instructions

Preparatory section (Rows 1-2)
1. Add a row of the twisted knit stitch and an anchor.
2. Add a row of the double rib stitch and knit off loop pairs.

Repeat section (four rows of the double rib stitch) (Rows 1-4)
1. Add a row of the double rib stitch. On the FR, double loop every second, fifth, and fourth peg thereafter.
2. Four-loop cross x-crosses
    a. Inner right cross
        i. Lift off the loop with a superscript 2 (e.g., pegs 4 and 8 on the FR).
        ii. Move the loop with a superscript 1 one peg to the right (e.g., pegs 3 and 7 on the FR).
        iii. Move the loop with a superscript 2 one peg to the left.
    b. Outer right cross
        i. Lift off the loop with the superscript 4 (e.g., pegs 5 and 9 on the FR).
        ii. Move the loop with a superscript 3 (e.g., pegs 2 and 6) to the peg with the superscript 4 (e.g., pegs 5 and 9).
        iii. Move the loop with a superscript 4 (e.g., pegs 5 and 9) to the peg with the superscript 3 (e.g., pegs 2 and 6).
3. Add three to five rows of the double rib stitch.

End section (Rows 1-2)
1. Add a row of the double rib stitch and double loop every second, fifth, and fourth peg thereafter on the FR.
2. Add an outer four-loop right cross (see Repeat section 2b).
3. Add a row of the double rib stitch.

Figure 104: A standard four-loop cable and an x-cross cable©.

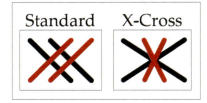

Figure 105: Knitting chart for the x-cross rib cable©.

58 · The Easier Way to Knit

Brioche stitches

The brioche knitting technique creates a highly textured, elastic double knit fabric with vertical ribs on one side and either a contrasting flat stitch or a raised rib stitch on the other side, depending on the pattern used on the BR. Multicolor brioche stitches with harmonizing or contrasting colors are especially beautiful and are an excellent medium for raised cables. Using knitting needles, brioche knitting is an advanced technique that uses tucked stitches, which slips loops from multiple rows onto a stitch. Fortunately, tucked stitches are easier to knit on a double rake loom than with knitting needles.

Stockinette brioche with fish-scales

Figure 106 summaries how to knit a solid color stockinette brioche stitch with raised ribs on the front and a fish-scale pattern on the back. The knitting chart and swatch for this stitch are illustrated in Figure 107 and Figure 108. The brioche stitch is unique because the stitches on each rake are knit differently. The raised ribs on the FR are formed with tucked stitches that are knit off whenever there are three loops on a peg and the fish-scale pattern on the BR is formed by knitting off loop pairs.

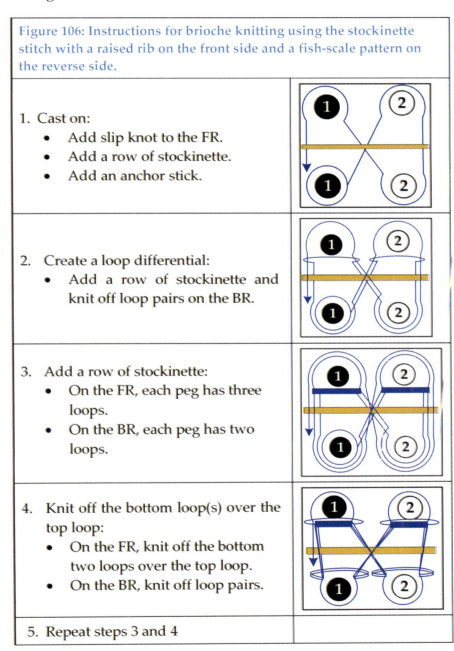

Figure 106: Instructions for brioche knitting using the stockinette stitch with a raised rib on the front side and a fish-scale pattern on the reverse side.

1. Cast on:
   - Add slip knot to the FR.
   - Add a row of stockinette.
   - Add an anchor stick.

2. Create a loop differential:
   - Add a row of stockinette and knit off loop pairs on the BR.

3. Add a row of stockinette:
   - On the FR, each peg has three loops.
   - On the BR, each peg has two loops.

4. Knit off the bottom loop(s) over the top loop:
   - On the FR, knit off the bottom two loops over the top loop.
   - On the BR, knit off loop pairs.

5. Repeat steps 3 and 4

Stitches • 59

Figure 107: Knitting chart for a stockinette brioche with a raised rib on the front side and a fish-scale pattern on the back.

Figure 108: Stockinette brioche with a raised rib on the front side of the fabric and a fish-scale pattern on the reverse side.

Repeat	●	●	●	●	2 FR
	●	●	●	●	1 BR
	○	○	○	○	1 FR
Prep	○	○	○	○	1
	1	2	3	4	

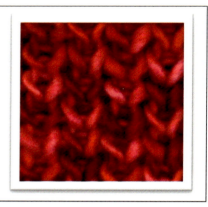

Brioche knitting tips

1. To form a smooth edge, hold the loose strand(s) against the rake when knitting off the first peg.
2. After knitting off the first stitch on the FR, tighten the loop by securing the lower yarn strand.
3. To prevent stretching, use a smooth self-sticking yarn, such as smooth worsted wool, and avoid superwash yarn, which is not smooth.
4. The brioche stitch requires more yarn than other double knit stitches.
5. Increase and decrease stitches in pairs.
6. When estimating gauge, use the raised rib side of the fabric to count stitches per cm because these stitches are easier to count than the fish-scale pattern on the back of the fabric.

Two-color brioche

Figure 109 illustrates the knitting chart for a two-color stockinette brioche fabric with raised red ribs on the front side of the fabric and a predominately blue fish-scale pattern on the reverse side. The first two rows of the brioche stitch (prep row 1 + repeat row 1) form the background color for the raised rib and the dominant color for the fish-scale pattern.

Figure 109: Knitting chart for a two-color stockinette brioche with ribs on one side and fish-scales on the reverse side.

Repeat	●	●	●	●	2 FR
	●	●	●	●	1 BR
	○	○	○	○	1 FR
Prep	○	○	○	○	1
	1	2	3	4	

Knitting instructions

1) Add a row of stockinette using the background color.
2) Add an anchor stick.
3) Add another row of stockinette with the background color and knit off loop pairs on the BR.
4) With a slip stitch, attach a second yarn to the first peg and add a row of stockinette.
5) On the BR, knit off loop pairs and on the FR, knit off the bottom two loops over the top loop each time there are three loops on a peg.
6) Repeat steps 3-5.

While two color brioche knitting is similar to the one-color variety, forming smooth edges with multiple color yarns requires diligence as detailed in Figure 110.

Figure 110: Instructions for a two-color stockinette brioche with ribs on one side and fish-scales on the reverse side.

1. Add two wraps of the stockinette stitch with one color • Add slip knot to front rake. • Wrap pegs with the first yarn (blue yarn). • Add an anchor. • Add a second wrap with the first yarn (blue yarn). • Knit-off loops on back peg (and after every wrap).	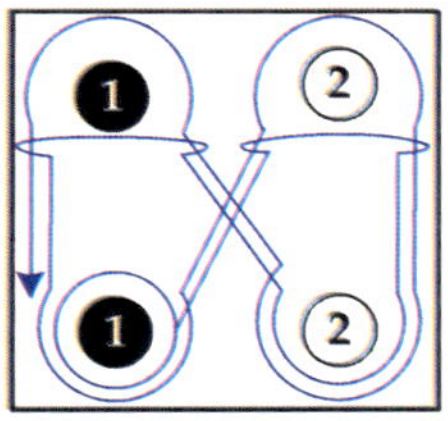
2. Wrap pegs with a harmonizing color (second yarn) • Attach the second yarn (red yarn) to front rake with a slip knot. • Wrap pegs (front pegs have three loops and back pegs have two loops).	
3. Add a stitch to the front and back sides of the fabric • Front pegs: Knit-off the two bottom (blue) loops over the top red loop. • Back pegs: Knit-off loops.	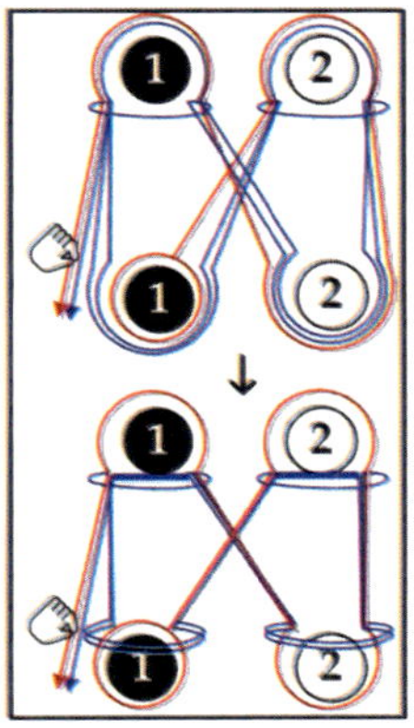
4. Wrap pegs with the first yarn (blue yarn) • Bring first yarn strand (blue yarn) over the second yarn strand (red yarn). • Wrap yarn around pegs. • Back pegs: Knit-off loops.	
5. Wrap pegs with second color yarn (red yarn) • Bring second yarn strand (red yarn) over first yarn strand (blue yarn). • Bring first yarn strand (blue yarn) over second yarn strand (red yarn). • Wrap second color yarn (red yarn). • Front pegs: Knit-off bottom two loops over top loop (hold yarn strands tautly when looping first peg). • Back pegs: Knit-off loops.	
6. Wrap pegs with the first yarn (blue yarn) like steps 4 • Uncross yarn strands. • Wrap yarn around pegs. • Back pegs: Knit-off loops.	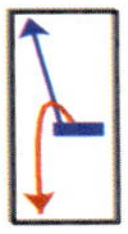
7. Repeat step 5 and 6.	

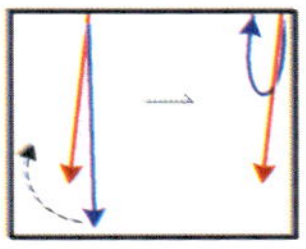

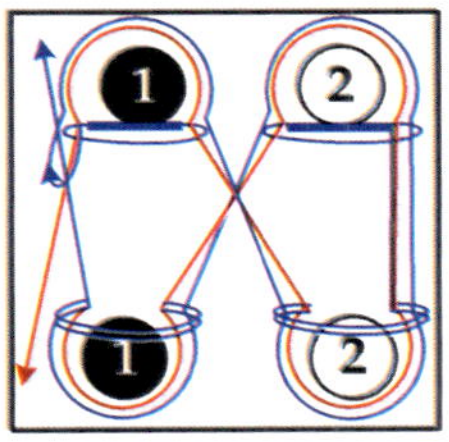

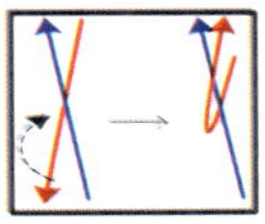

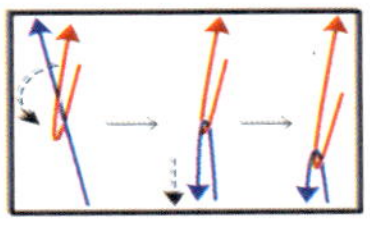

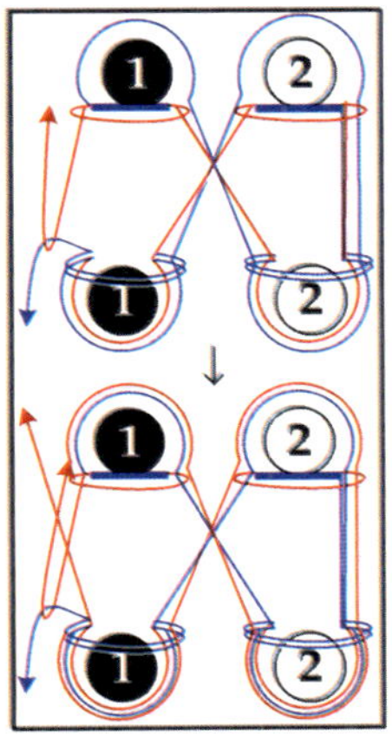

Stitches • 61

Color

Brioche knitting is a great medium for gorgeous color plays between the fabric's raised ribs and recessed background. Many factors influence the color plays between the two levels. These factors include the physical properties of color and vision, such as the effect of adjacent colors, color harmonies, the proportion of each color, the color's wavelength, the width of adjacent colors, and even illusions due to the vertical and horizontal stitches. These effects are dramatically illustrated when the rib and background colors of two stockinette brioche fabrics are reversed, as illustrated in the teal and white fabrics in Figure 111. In this example, the white ribs pop off the dark teal background (fabric 1) while the reverse color combination (fabric 2) is dull and muted. This occurs because it is harder for the eye to differentiate dark or deep pigments than lighter ones. A similar affect is visible in the fish-scale pattern; the predominately teal fish-scales create a muted fabric while the predominately white fish-scales create a vibrant, clearly attenuated pattern.

Figure 111: Reverse colors on stockinette brioche fabric with a raised rib on one side and a fish-scale pattern on the reverse side.

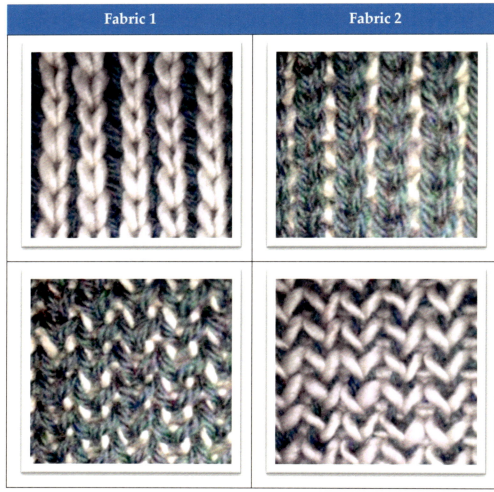

Stockinette brioche with reverse color ribs

Figure 112 illustrates a knitting chart for a stockinette brioche fabric with red ribs on the front side of the fabric and blue ribs on the reverse side. Each side of the fabric looks very different because the recessed background color affects how the raised ribs in the foreground are perceived.

Figure 112: Knitting chart for a two-color stockinette brioche with ribs on both sides of the fabric.

62 · The Easier Way to Knit

Right crosses on stockinette brioche©

Two-color stockinette brioche can be used to create beautiful raised cables that swirl on top of a contrasting or a harmonizing base, such as the accompanying swatch. The looping technique for this stitch is identical to the two-color stockinette brioche with the addition of right crosses after the preparatory stitches and after every fourth rib stitch. Figure 113 illustrates the knitting chart for this multistep stitch.

Knitting instructions

Preparatory section
1. Cast on with the stockinette stitch (Rows 1-3):
    a. Weave a row of stockinette with the recessed color and add an anchor.
    b. Weave a second row of stockinette with the recessed color and knit off loops on the BR.
    c. Add a row of stockinette with the color of the raised ribs and knit off bottom loop(s) on both the FR and the BR.
    d. Add a row of right crosses:
        i. Lift off first and second loops.
        ii. Move first loop onto the second peg (e.g., move the loop that was on peg 3 to peg 4).
        iii. Move second loop onto the first peg (e.g., move the loop that was on peg 4 to peg 3).

Repeat section (Rows 1-6)
1. Add three rows of stockinette brioche (steps 1-6).
2. Add a row of right crosses (see 1d).

Figure 113: Knitting chart for right crosses on two color stockinette brioche©.

Stitches • 63

Spiral rib on stockinette brioche©

The spiral rib is a dynamic, multistep rib stitch that is created by alternating left and right crosses after every other pair of rib stitches. Figure 114 illustrates the knitting chart for this stitch. Each pair of spiral ribs requires two rows per spiral and four stitches (a two-stitch right cross and a two-stitch left cross) per spiral pair. Therefore, this stitch requires multiples of four stitches and an even number of rows.

Knitting instructions

Preparatory section (Row 1)

Cast on with a row of stockinette using the recessed color yarn and add an anchor.

Repeat section (Rows 1-3)

1. Add a row of stockinette brioche:
    a. Add a row of stockinette with the recessed color yarn and knit off loops on the BR.
    b. Add a row of stockinette with the color of the spiral ribs and knit off bottom loop(s) on both rakes.
    c. Alternate between left and right crosses on every pair of pegs (e.g., left crosses on pegs 1 and 2, 5 and 6, etc. and right crosses on pegs 3 and 4, 7 and 8, etc.).
        1. Directions for cross
            1. Lift off first and second loops.
            2. Move first loop to second peg.
            3. Move second loop to first peg.

Figure 114: Knitting chart for the spiral rib stitch©.

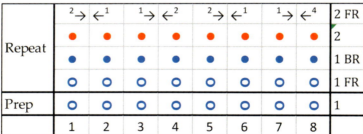

English brioche

English brioche with raised fish-scales

The decorative and elastic English (a.k.a. waffle) brioche is a versatile stitch that is both decorative and elastic. To knit this stitch, apply the brioche knitting technique to the English stitch. The resulting fabric is like a stockinette brioche. However, English brioche has a wider and more distinct recessed pattern than a stockinette brioche. Also, unlike the stockinette brioche stitch, which has a similar recessed pattern regardless of the pattern on the BR, the recessed stitches for English brioche differ greatly depending on the knitting pattern on the BR. The English brioche pattern with a fish-scale pattern on the back of the fabric creates wide, flat slip stitches that looks like isosceles triangles as illustrated in Figure 115.

Figure 115

The knitting chart for a two-color English brioche fabric with raised fish-scales is illustrated in Figure 116. This chart corresponds to a fabric with blue ribs and recessed red stitches on the front side of the fabric and a predominantly red fish-scale pattern on the back of the fabric. Knit this stitch on an odd number of pegs. Knit odd pegs on the FR and even pegs on the BR using the brioche knitting technique. On the BR, knit off every row of stitches, and on the FR, knit off the two bottom loops every time there are three loops on a peg. Tip: To prevent loopy stitches, knit tightly.

Knitting instructions

Preparatory section (Rows 1)

1. Cast on with recessed color yarn and add an anchor.

Repeat section (Rows 1-2)

1. Weave one row of the English stitch using the recessed color and knit off loop pairs on the BR.
2. Weave one row of the English stitch using the rib color. On the BR, knit off loop pairs, and on the FR, knit off two bottom loops over the top loop.

Figure 116: Knitting chart for a two-color English brioche with a raised rib on the front and a fish-scale pattern on the reverse side.

	1	2	3	4	5	6	7	
Repeat		•		•		•		2 BR
	•		•		•		•	2 FR
		•		•		•		1 BR
	○		○		○		○	1 FR
Prep		○		○		○		1 BR
	○		○		○		○	1 FR

English brioche with accordion ribs

The English brioche stitch with raised ribs on both sides of the fabric is deeply recessed with accordion-like pleats. The pleats occur because the vertical bar between each pair of angled slip stitches is narrower at the base than at the top of the stitch. Figure 117 illustrates the knitting chart for a fabric with blue ribs on the front and red ribs on the back. Knit this stitch on an odd number of pegs and cast on with the English brioche stitch. Tip: To prevent loopy stitches, knit tightly.

Knitting instructions

Preparatory section (Row 1)
1. Cast on with recessed color yarn and add an anchor.

Repeat section (Rows 1-2)
1. Weave one row of the English stitch using the recessed color and knit off bottom loop(s) on the BR.
2. Weave one row of the English stitch using the rib color and knit off the bottom loop(s) over the top loop on the FR.

Figure 117: Knitting chart for the English brioche with raised ribs on both sides of the fabric.

66 · The Easier Way to Knit

Fretwork stitches

Fretwork stitches are stitches with an interlaced decorative design. In addition to the stitches in this section, the little bee stitch is also a fretwork stitch.

Closed Braid stitch

The closed braid (a.k.a. cat's tail) stitch has narrow plaited columns separated by narrow horizontal slip stitches. This stitch is 10 percent narrower than its wrap sequence. This nonelastic stitch requires an even number of stitches per row with a minimum of four stitches. The knitting chart for this stitch is shown in Figure 118.

Cast on: Attach a slip knot around peg 8 (BR), add a row of the twisted knit stitch, and an anchor.

Forward wrap: Loop yarn counterclockwise on the FR and clockwise on the BR. To begin the forward wrap, weave the yarn from the first peg on the BR, down to the left of the third peg on the FR and up to the left of the second peg on the BR. Hereafter, weave every other peg on both rakes until the third to the last peg on the BR. To complete the forward wrap, weave the yarn down to the left of the last peg on the FR and straight across to the opposite peg.

Begin
1. Attach a slip knot around peg 1 (BR).

Repeat
1. Weave the yarn to left of peg 3 (FR) and counterclockwise around it.
2. Weave the yarn up to the left of peg 2 (BR) and clockwise around it.
3. Weave the yarn down to the left of peg 5 (FR) and counterclockwise around.

End
1. Weave the yarn counterclockwise around peg 8 (BR) and bring the yarn straight up to the BR.

Return wrap: The return wrap transverses the same pattern as the forwad wrap but in the opposite direction.

Figure 118: Knitting chart for the closed braid stitch.

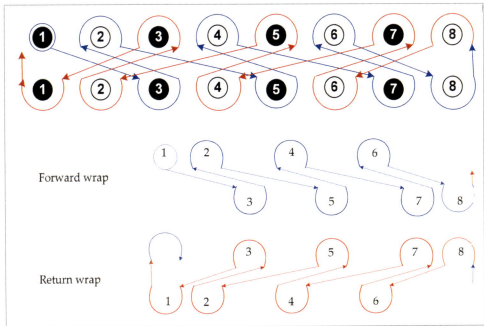

Stitches • 67

Slide stitch

The slide stitch is a slightly elastic tubular rib stitch with angular slip stitches. This stitch is 30 percent narrower than its wrap sequence. It requires an even number of stitches and a cast-on stitch that loops each peg. The forward and return wrap sequences are illustrated in Figure 119. However, the looping diagram for this multidirectional stitch is not included because the overlapping wraps are difficult to see.

Cast on: Add a slip knot to peg 2 on the BR, add a row of the slide stitch, and add an anchor.

Forward wrap: Loop yarn counterclockwise on odd pegs on both rakes and clockwise on even pegs on both rakes, except for peg 2 (FR), which is looped counterclockwise.

Begin
1. Weave the yarn straight down to the left of peg 2 (FR) and counterclockwise around it.

Repeat
1. Weave the yarn up to the left side of peg 2 (BR) and clockwise around it.
2. Weave the yarn down to the left of peg 1 (FR) and counterclockwise around it.
3. Weave the yarn up to the right of peg 1 (BR) and counterclockwise around it.
4. Weave the yarn down to the right of peg 4 (FR) and clockwise around it.
5. Weave the yarn up to the left of peg 4 (BR) and clockwise around it.

End
1. Weave the yarn counterclockwise around peg 5 (BR) and down to the right side of it.

Return wrap: The return wrap uses the same pattern as the forward wrap but in the opposite direction.

Begin
1. Weave the yarn clockwise around peg 5 (FR).
2. Weave the yarn up to the right side of peg 5 (BR) and counterclockwise around it.

Repeat
1. Weave the yarn down to the right of peg 6 (FR) and clockwise around it.
2. Weave the yarn up to the left of peg 6 (BR) and clockwise around it.
3. Weave the yarn down to the left of peg 3 (FR) and counterclockwise around it.
4. Weave the yarn up to the right side of peg 3 (BR) and counterclockwise around it.

End
1. Weave the yarn counterclockwise around peg 2 (BR).

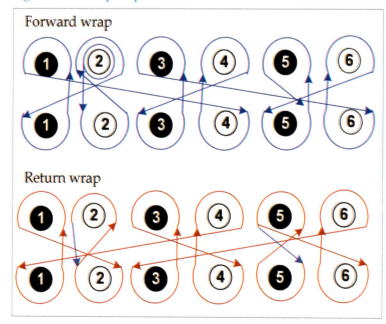

Figure 119: Wrap sequence for the slide stitch.

68 · The Easier Way to Knit

Large honeycomb tube stitch©

The large honeycomb tube stitch is a laterally elastic compound stitch that includes four rows of the slide stitch followed by two rows of the closed braid stitch. Cast on with the twisted knit stitch. The knitting chart and looping diagrm for this stitch are illustrated in Figure 120 and Figure 121.

Cast on: Add a slip stitch to peg 8 (BR), add one rotation of the twisted knit stitch, and add an anchor.

Figure 120: Knitting chart for the large honeycomb tube stitch©.

End	S	S	S	S
	S	S	S	S
	S	S	S	S
	S	S	S	S
Repeat	C	C	C	C
	C	C	C	C
	S	S	S	S
	S	S	S	S
	S	S	S	S
	S	S	S	S
Prep	8	8	8	8
	1	2	3	4

Pattern sequence:
1. Rows 1-4: Slide stitch.
2. Rows 5-6: Closed braid stitch.
3. End 1-4: Slide stitch.

Figure 121: Lopping diagram for the large honeycomb tubes stitch©.

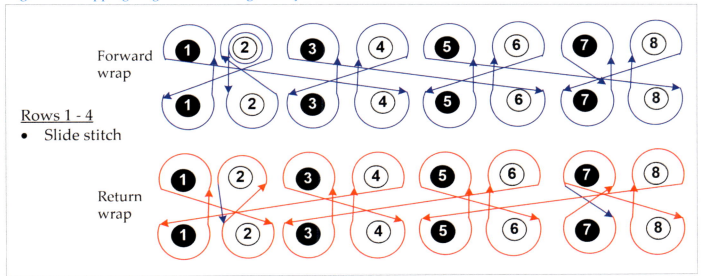

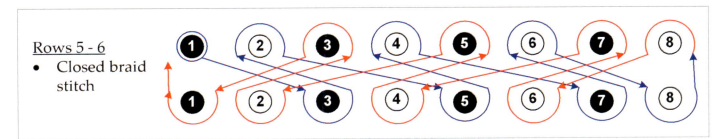

Stitches • 69

Small honeycomb tube stitch©

The small honeycomb tube stitch© is a latteraly elastic compound stitch that is knit with two rows of the closed braid stitch followed by two rows of the slide stitch. Cast on with the twisted knit stitch. The knitting chart and looping diagrm for this stitch are illustrated in Figure 122 and Figure 123.

Figure 122: Knitting chart for the small honeycomb tube stitch©.

End	S	S	S	S
	S	S	S	S
Repeat	C	C	C	C
	C	C	C	C
	S	S	S	S
	S	S	S	S
Prep	8	8	8	8
	1	2	3	4

Cast on: Add a slip stitch to peg 8 (BR), add one rotation of the twisted knit stitch, and add an anchor.

Pattern sequence
1. Rows 1-2: Slide stitch.
2. Rows 3-4: Closed braid stitch.
3. End 1-2: Slide stitch.

Figure 123: Lopping diagram for the small honeycomb tube stitch©.

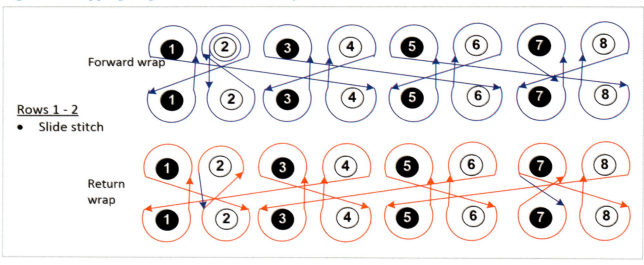

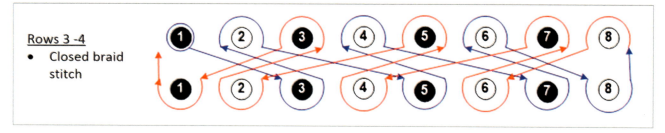

70 · The Easier Way to Knit

Narrow tube stitch©

The narrow tube stitch© is knit with a figure 8 cast on followed by rows of the double figure 8 stitch. This nonelastic stitch is the same width as its wrap sequence. The looping diagram for this stitch is illustrated in Figure 124.

Cast on: Add a slip knot onto peg 8 (BR), a figure 8 cast on, and an anchor.

Forward wrap: Loop yarn counterclockwise on the BR and clockwise on the FR.

Repeat
1. Weave the yarn up to the right of peg 2 (BR) and counterclockwise around pegs 1 and 2 (BR).
2. Weave the yarn down to the right of peg 2 (FR) and clockwise around pegs 1 and 2 (FR).
3. Weave the yarn up to the right of peg 4 (BR) and counterclockwise around pegs 3 and 4 (BR).

End
1. After looping the last pair of pegs on the FR, weave the yarn straight up to the BR (left of peg 7) and begin the return wrap.

Return wrap uses the same pattern as the forward wrap but in the opposite direction. That forces clockwise loops on the BR and counterclockwise loops on the FR.

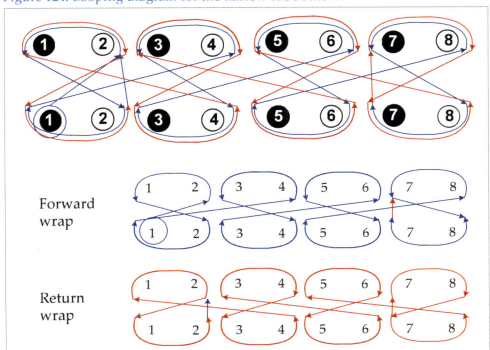

Figure 124: Looping diagram for the narrow tube stitch©.

Stitches • 71

Index

basic stitches
double knit stitch, 8, 46
English stitch, 43
fashion stitch, 14, 44
little bee stitch, 47
single rib stitch, 44
slant-u stitch, 44
stockinette stitch, 3, 13, 41
stripes, 32
twisted knit stitch, 46
twisted rib stitch, 46
twisted stockinette stitch, 3, 16, 42
waffle stitch, 14, 43, 64
zigzag stitch, 45

binding off
elastic loom hook bind-off, 9-10
fringe, 11
loom hook, 10
narrow crochet, 9

brioche
English brioche, 65-66
fish scale pattern, 60
gauge, 60
right crosses on stockinette
brioche©, 40, 63
simple brioche, 35
spiral rib stitch©, 40, 64
stockinette brioche, 59-62
two color brioche, 60-66

casting on
anchor, 5
fringe, 8
slip knot, 3, 4
tight cast-on, 6

color knitting
basic color techniques, 32
beading, 15-6, 31, 38-39
color theory, 31
intarsia, 31, 34
simple brioche, 31, 35
stranded knitting, 31
stripes, 32
tangrams, 31

conventions
knitoglyphics, 21-22, 24-25
knitting chart, iv, 21-5
looping diagrams, 2

crosses
cables, 23, 40, 53-54, 57-58, 63-64
double right cross, 23
elongated slip stitch, 24-26
notation, 24-25
one-three cross 53-54
right crosses, 23-4, 30, 63-64
x-cross, 40, 58

custom fit
gauge, 1, 16-18, 30, 35, 60
rows to knit, 18-20
pegs to wrap, 18-20
yarn calculator/estimator, 19-20

double knit fabric
interlocking, iv, 1
loop structure, 13
structure, 13, 15

fretwork stitches
cat's tail, 67
closed braid stitch, 67
large honeycomb tube stitch©, 40,
69
narrow tube stitch©, 40, 71
slide stitch, 68
small honeycomb tube stitch©, 40,
70

gauge, See custom fit

knitting techniques
adding a keyhole, 29
adding a buttonhole, 29
beading, 15, 31, 38-39
changing yarn, 27
color knitting, iv, 31-39, 60-66
compound stitches, 26, 69-70
fringe, 8, 11
invisible seams, 30
knitting stitches, 8
shaping, 28

loop types
e-wrap, 3
u-wrap, 3

rib stitches
alligator stitch, 50
Andaluz chain stitch with
beads©, 38, 40, 51
Andaluz stitch, 50
box stitch, 49
cable rib stitch, 57
double rib stitch, 56
double rib stitch variation, 56
raised rib stitch©, 40, 48
ribbing stitch, 56
single rib stitch, 44
slipped tube stitch©, 40, 55
twisted double rib stitch, 49
twisted knit stitch, 46
wide rib cable©, 21, 25, 40, 53
wide rib cable with beads©, 40,
54
wide rib stich, 25, 52-54
x-cross rib cable©, 40, 58

slip stitches
cross angles, 14
elasticity, 14
elongated slip stitches, 242-6
tucked stitches, 21, 23, 59
twisted slip stitch, 32-36

tools
double rake loom, 1
loom hook, 7-8
stylus, 12

About the Author

As early as she can remember, Kera Weiserbs has been involved with craft arts like knitting. She majored in Materials Arts at Oberlin College and has a PhD in Epidemiology from Johns Hopkins University. Kera's unique background in art, mathematics, and science helped her develop systematic methods for understanding the structure of and representation of double loom knit stitches.

Made in the USA
Lexington, KY
26 April 2018